Aphorisms of Gustave Le Bon:
A Sampler

Crowds respect only the strong. Disdain for the weak is their law.

To excuse evil is to multiply it.

It is not necessary to multiply gods. Under various names, man has adored during all the ages only one divinity—hope.

Only people with lots of cannons have the right to be pacifists.

The only lasting revolutions are those of thought.

The first task of a revolution is to destroy the old aristocracy; the second is to create a new one.

The role of the scholar is to destroy chimeras, that of the statesman is to make use of them.

A leader is seldom in advance of public opinion; almost always all he does is follow it and espouse all its errors.

Science still is full of shadows and, behind the horizons it has attained, others appear, lost in an infinity which seems ever to recede.

One does not behave according to one's intelligence but according to one's character.

In politics, things are less important than their names. To disguise even the most absurd ideas with well-chosen words often is enough to gain their acceptance.

For a copy of our catalog, write: Liberty*Press*/Liberty*Classics*, 7440 North Shadeland, Indianapolis, Indiana 46250.

Gustave Le Bon

(continued from front flap)

"Today," concludes Mrs. Widener, "it would seem Le Bon can best be compared to Sir Francis Bacon. Le Bon's mind, like Bacon's, ranged over many fields of science and psychology, illuminating and interpreting them for widest possible appreciation. His enemies, like Bacon's, belittled him as a mere 'popularizer' or 'vulgarizer.' Both Bacon and Le Bon strove to weld knowledge of nature and man into an integrated, useful whole. Admiring the best of Aristotle and Machiavelli, they took no theories or concepts for granted, not even those of the physical sciences, and based their philosophy on practicality rather than idealism."

Alice Widener is a syndicated columnist on national and international affairs and publisher of *U.S.A.* magazine, which she founded in 1954. She is fluent  in French and several other languages, and was educated privately as a young girl in Paris and Rome under the tutelage of Emilie Thouvenel and Professor Luigi Valli, who held the Chair of Dante at the University of Rome. Mrs. Widener is author of *Teachers of Destruction*, and her writings have appeared in *Life, Atlantic Monthly, Revue Musicale, The Freeman, Barron's,* and many other publications. *Editor & Publisher* has cited her "outstanding record for discerning trends and reporting them" and describes her column as "often ahead of others in interpreting developments." She is a member of the Mont Pelerin Society.

Liberty*Press* is a publishing imprint of Liberty Fund, Inc., a foundation established to encourage study of the ideal of a society of free and responsible individuals.

Le Bon's tomb in Père Lachaise Cemetery, Paris

Gustave Le Bon
The Man and His Works

A Presentation with Introduction,
first translations into
English, and edited extracts
by Alice Widener

Liberty*Press*

Indianapolis

Liberty*Press* is a publishing imprint of Liberty Fund, Inc., a foundation established to encourage study of the ideal of a society of free and responsible individuals.

The cuneiform inscription that serves as the design motif for our endpapers is the earliest known written appearance of the word "freedom" (*ama-gi*), or liberty. It is taken from a clay document written about 2300 B.C. in the Sumerian city-state of Lagash.

Library of Congress Cataloging in Publication Data

Le Bon, Gustave, 1841–1931.
  Gustave Le Bon, the man and his works.

  Le Bon's works are translated from French. Includes index.
  1. Social psychology—Addresses, essays, lectures. 2. Le Bon, Gustave, 1841–1931. 3. Crowds—Addresses, essays, lectures. I. Widener, Alice. II. Title.
HM251.L338   301.1   78–14774
ISBN 0–913966–50–9

With gratitude and affection,
I dedicate this book to my friend
Donald H. Ludwig of St. Louis, Missouri,
who introduced me to the works
of Gustave Le Bon.

Contents

Acknowledgments

For their courtesy and helpfulness in the research for this book, I wish to express my deepest appreciation to Vidiane Koechlin-Schwartz, Librarian, Public Library, Nogent-le-Rotrou, France; to the directors of the Bibliothèque Royale, Brussels, Belgium, and the Bibliothèque Nationale, Paris, France; to Cultural Counselor Pierre Tabatoni, permanent representative of the Universities of France, French Embassy, New York City; to Monique Polgar, Press Officer, French Embassy, New York City; and to my assistant LeRoy Sluder III.

Introduction
By Alice Widener

Why, in this the age of mass media and mass education, is the name of Gustave Le Bon, whose
works strongly influenced such disparate figures as
Lenin and Mussolini, Theodore Roosevelt and Sigmund
Freud, largely unknown? How can most of the psychological, philosophical, and scientific works of such
a genius as Le Bon be largely ignored or blanketed by a
"conspiracy of silence"? That is the term used by his
close friend Edmond Picard, eminent Belgian jurist,
who described Le Bon as "homo multiplex"—a man of
manifold genius.[1]

Le Bon is the undisputed founder of social psychology. His book *The Psychology of the Crowd* (1895)
laid the foundations for the study of mass human
action. His *The Evolution of Matter* (1896) and *The*

---

[1] Edmond Picard, "Gustave Le Bon et son Oeuvre," *Mercure de France* (Paris, 1909).

Evolution of Forces (1907) prophesied our nuclear era. Before 1905 Le Bon perceived the theory of relativity but did not prove it by mathematical equation. He originated and stimulated valuable research into radiation. In political science his two great works *The Psychology of Socialism* and *The Psychology of Revolutions* predicted not only the worldwide advance of socialism but almost all its now-apparent social, political, and economic consequences.

From his birth in Nogent-le-Rotrou, France, on May 7, 1841, until his death at Marne-la-Coquette near Paris, on December 13, 1931, Le Bon never ceased to grow in powers of observation and interpretation. Every place to which he traveled, every event he took part in or witnessed, including the Franco-Prussian War of 1870, the Paris Commune of 1871, and World War I, every incident or accident he observed or suffered, inspired and stimulated him.

In 1892, for example, he narrowly escaped death when thrown from the high-spirited horse he was riding. Instead of blaming the animal, he began to study what he had done wrong as a rider. The result was his *Equitation: The Psychology of the Horse,* containing two hundred photographs taken by himself of horses in action, an entirely new interpretation of horse training, and a system of rules for it. The work became a classic cavalry manual for top military establishments in France and abroad, and also an invaluable guide for horse breeders and trainers throughout the world. Just as his great Russian contemporary Ivan Pavlov used his studies of dogs' conditioned reflexes to apply to human behavior, so Le Bon used his studies of horses to develop theories of child education.

Paradoxically, Le Bon is a main prophet and victim of twentieth-century intellectual life in which philosophy, science, and art have been largely distorted and corrupted by ideology. Most sociologists today ignore Le Bon's teachings because his views run counter to theirs. The only work of Le Bon's still taught at many universities is his *The Psychology of the Crowd*.

In 1954, Professor Gordon W. Allport of Harvard University, an eminent American sociologist, described *The Crowd* as perhaps "the most influential book ever written in social psychology."[2] According to Professor Robert K. Merton of Columbia University, when Sigmund Freud in the 1930s turned his attention to group psychology and published his first monograph on the subject, he cited Le Bon's *The Psychology of the Crowd* as a "brilliantly executed picture of the group mind."[3]

Contemporary singling out of Le Bon's *The Crowd* for attention and almost complete disregard of his other great psychological and philosophical works is comparable to singling out Beethoven's *Eroica* and ignoring his eight other symphonies.

Until his death in 1931 Le Bon's best sellers were

---

[2] Gordon W. Allport, "The Historical Background of Modern Psychology," ed. Gardner Lindzey (Reading, Mass.: Addison-Wesley, 1954), p. 26.

[3] Gustave Le Bon, *The Crowd*, introd. by Robert K. Merton (New York: Viking Press, 1969), p. vii.

sold and read widely in his native France and abroad. The day after his death, the *Journal des Débats,* most highly regarded political and literary newspaper in Paris at that time, reported on its front page: "In putting an end to the long, diverse and fruitful activity of Gustave Le Bon, death deprived our culture of a truly remarkable man. His was a most exceptional mind; he was a man of exceptional intelligence; it sprang entirely from within himself; he was his own master, his own initiator. . . . Science and philosophy have suffered a cruel loss."

The *New York Times* said in its obituary:

> Dr. Le Bon was for many years one of the foremost men of science in Europe. He was Professor of Psychology and Allied Sciences at the University of Paris. . . . His scientific investigations of tobacco smoke, skulls, photographic surveys, the laws of matter and motion, indicate the versatility of his erudition.
>
> It is, however, as a psychologist that civilization is chiefly indebted to Dr. Le Bon. . . . His book *The Psychology of Modern Times*, published some time ago, was said by the American press to have "astounded the entire world of science."
>
> It was in the years immediately after the close of the World War that Dr. Le Bon became known to Americans. His following in this country included the late President Theodore Roosevelt and later, former Vice President [Charles] Dawes. . . .

Suddenly, it seemed a silence enveloped Gustave Le Bon, although the world had saluted his genius.

In a doctoral thesis, Dr. Robert Allen Nye, professor of political science at the University of Oklahoma, offers the following reasons for the almost complete disregard of Le Bon in France since 1931:

> First, he was a violent enemy of the French scientific establishment which had never accepted any of his far-reaching scientific work save *The Psychology of the Crowd* as authoritative, and it chose to destroy him through silence; secondly, after the Second World War, the political climate of republican and leftist dominance was hardly favorable to a sympathetic study of his conservative philosophy.
>
> Most social scientists carried along strong political and social commitments, and still do, in their studies, seriously prejudicing their conclusions and jeopardizing the objectivity after which all science worthy of the name should strive.[4]

Actually, the "conspiracy of silence" had been under way much earlier than Professor Nye indicates. In 1906 Professor Henri Lorent, mathematician and director of Teachers College at Charleroi, Belgium, wrote:

> Dr. Gustave Le Bon recently published a summary of the theories which he has issued during several years on diverse physical and chemical phenomena [*The Evolution of Matter*]. These theories have been the object in certain circles of a disdainful silence; in others, of enthusiastic praise.

---

[4] Robert Allen Nye, *An Intellectual Portrait of Gustave Le Bon: A Study of the Development and Impact of a Social Scientist in His Historical Setting* (Ann Arbor, Mich.: Xerox University Microfilms, 1969), p. 5.

As a general rule, official scientific circles seem to ignore the existence of Le Bon's work. The French Physics Society, under the direction of Messrs. H. Abraham and P. Langevin, got together the compendium of papers relative to *Elementary Quantities of Electricity* (ions, electrons, particles); the works of Le Bon are not mentioned. At the Conference of the Study of Radiology and Ionization held at Liège [Belgium] in September 1905, the name of Le Bon was not once pronounced, though his works contain, so to say, the essence of most of the comunications made to the Conference. The Science Section of the Belgian Academy did itself the honor of refusing to take part in this conspiracy of silence and named Dr. Le Bon as associate member.

On the other hand, following De Heen [Professor of Physics] of the University of Liège, who was first to render justice to Le Bon, diverse independent scholars and several sagacious critics heralded the importance of the research he has done and the ideas he put forth.[5]

Dr. Lorent went on to cite the following quotations:

F. Legge, Royal Institution of Great Britain, *The Athenaeum,* July 8, 1905: "The research of Gustave Le Bon will certainly be considered as having the same importance on the twentieth century as that of Darwin on the nineteenth."

J. Sageret, *Revue Philosophique,* Paris, France, November 1, 1905: "One should give to Dr. Gustave Le

---

[5] Henri Lorent, "The Theories of Doctor G. Le Bon on The Evolution of Matter," *Bulletin of the Belgian Chemical Society* 20, nos. 1-2 (January-February 1906).

Bon, in the physical sciences, the place that Darwin occupies in natural history. . . ."

Le Bon conducted his experiments in physics and chemistry during the period 1896–1908 in a laboratory at home, in Paris, with apparatus often designed by him. As early as 1902 and 1903, he wrote about "the manifestations of a new force—namely intra-atomic energy —which surpasses all others by its colossal magnitude." Le Bon pondered the dissociation of matter, upsetting many theories supposed to be scientific facts, and he wondered about what would result "if radium or any other substance were dissociated rapidly instead of requiring centuries for the purpose." He said that a scholar who discovered the way to dissociate instantaneously one gram of any metal "will not witness the results of his experiment. The explosion produced would be so formidable that his laboratory and all the neighboring houses, with their inhabitants, would be instantaneously pulverized." Such a dissociation probably never would be attained, "yet there is hope that the partial dissociation of atoms may be rendered less slow."

Gustave Le Bon's descent into obscurity began immediately following publication of his book *The Psychology of Socialism* (1898). In it Le Bon described socialism as a new religion which promised heaven on earth and predicted that it would triumph throughout the world but would be the shortest lived of all religions because it could not fulfill its promises. Only collectivism and "total terror" would result.

Concerning Le Bon's analysis of socialism, Edmond Picard wrote:

> That is one of those subjects against which one burns one's wings unless they are incombustible, which seems to me to be the case of Gustave Le Bon. For the crime of having written that book, suppressed and reedited, he was despised by more than one great and by many little "devotees."[6]

Socialist "devotees" unable to refute Le Bon began belittling or ignoring him. In 1905 the French Society of Physics omitted his name from the compendium of studies on the elementary quantities of electricity issued under the direction of H. Abraham and Paul Langevin.[7]

Socialist hostility toward Le Bon intensified following publication of his *The Psychology of Revolutions* (1912). In it he argued that revolutions accomplish very little of a constructive nature; they destroy existing institutions only to replace them later under a

---

[6] Yet the French syndicalist Georges Sorel (1847–1922), with whom Le Bon had entered into the freest intellectual discussions, held that *The Psychology of Socialism* constituted "the most complete study published in France about socialism" and merited "study with greatest care because the author's ideas are always original and eminently suggestive."

[7] Coincidental or not, both scientists were "devotees" of socialism. In fact, Langevin became a communist.

different name. "The absolutism of Louis XIV," he wrote, "is now replaced by that of the labor union leaders."

Gustave Le Bon was most certainly antisocialist— but was he a conservative? The answer depends on individual interpretation: he was a progressive thinker, he eagerly disregarded shibboleths and shams, he searched avidly for the true nature of man and society. Like Sir Francis Bacon during the Renaissance, Le Bon opposed the narrow, rigidly hierarchical educational system of his times. He refused to accept whatever was written, even by the most eminent academicians, as gospel.

Upon completion of his medical studies at the Faculty of Medicine and of his internship at the Hôtel Dieu in Paris at age twenty-five, he decided not to become a practicing physician but to try to gain wisdom through personal experience and observation. He taught himself English and German, using William Shakespeare as preferred language authority. Taking each line of Shakespeare in English, he compared it with the best available French and German translations; eventually, he could read both English and German easily and gained a scholarly knowledge of both as well as a mastery of best literary style.

In the first decade of our century, several distinguished scientists and literary critics in Belgium, England, and France ranked Le Bon's genius with that of Charles Darwin, Isaac Newton, and Jean Baptiste

Lamarck. Today, in retrospect, it would seem Le Bon can best be compared to Sir Francis Bacon. Le Bon's mind, like Bacon's, ranged over many fields of science and psychology, illuminating and interpreting them for widest possible appreciation. His enemies, like Bacon's, belittled him as a mere "popularizer" or "vulgarizer."

Both Bacon and Le Bon strove to weld knowledge of nature and man into an integrated, useful whole. Admiring the best of Aristotle and Machiavelli, they took no theories or concepts for granted, not even those of the physical sciences, and based their philosophy on practicality rather than idealism.

Perhaps one aspect of his strong opposition to the French establishment is enough to assess Le Bon's general attitudes. Forcefully, sometimes tactlessly, and always fearlessly, Le Bon opposed the narrow existing system of classical education in France. He wanted France to follow the American example of education in mechanics, science, and agricultural technology which had been largely responsible for American prosperity, agricultural abundance, and technological progress. For example, two months before the outbreak of World War I, he discussed his aim of creating an American-type technological university in France with former President Theodore Roosevelt at a luncheon in Paris. After the war, in a letter to Le Bon,[8] Roosevelt

[8] Roosevelt to Le Bon, November 4, 1918, Letter of President Theodore Roosevelt, Library of Congress, Washington, D.C.

said he would gladly lend his moral support to Le Bon's educational plans if the French educational authorities gave their approval. That approval never was given. Le Bon's book *The Psychology of Education,* published in 1902 and containing several chapters on American education, rankled the French academic hierarchy. In it, he also predicted that the United States would become the economic leader of the world as a result of its varied educational advantages.

Le Bon traveled widely, and from his travels he gained valuable insights which he imparted in his books on India, Arabia, and Nepal, and in his *Psychological Laws of the Evolution of Peoples,* published in 1894. Theodore Roosevelt kept that book next to the Bible in his own room all during his presidency, and in that book Le Ben set forth his conceptions concerning race.

Le Bon's youthful study of medicine sparked an interest in physiology, biology, phrenology, and anthropology. Later travels abroad widened his understanding, and he began to modify some of his ideas. Then, as Le Bon became deeply involved in the scientific study of human psychology, he developed a profound and mature comprehension of the subject of race.

In 1927, when he was eighty-six years old, Le Bon wrote in the introduction to the twelfth French edition of his *Psychological Laws of the Evolution of Peoples:*

The role of race is too preponderant in the life of peoples to remain misunderstood. The most ancient religious books clearly reveal its power. Only revolutionaries oblivious of the past were able to contest its force. . . .

Very precise anthropological observations prove that in effect there are no pure races among civilized peoples. Without doubt a few areas in Africa and Asia still contain some pure races, but in Europe there exist only what I call "historic races." These are the result of various crossings due to the hazards of migrations and conquests. If their [historical races'] hereditary psychological character becomes quite stable, it is because the products of these crossings were submitted for centuries to a common life, implying common institutions and above all common interests.

Such influences—repeated since the epoch when the people, preserved from conquering invasions, had arrived at political unity—created the character of the current races. These characters are set today for most nations, though their birth does not at all go back to prehistoric ages.

The psychological characteristics of races being very different, they are differently impressed by the same exterior influences. This often brings about an absolute and reciprocal incomprehension. This incomprehension has become all the more apparent since development of rapid communications has put people into closer contact.

The first consequence of this rapprochement was to cause those psychological differences which separate people, and the divergencies in comprehension engendered by those differences, to explode.

The European war [World War I] has shown once again how deep are the dissimilarities in the mentality of peoples belonging to the same civilization who have for a long time exchanged ideas and have in common many interests.

Le Bon's ninety-year journey through life began at 5:30 A.M. at his parents' home, Rue Saint Hilaire,

Nogent-le-Rotrou. At the time of Gustave's birth, his mother, Annette Josephine Eugénic Tétiot Desmarlinais, was twenty-six. His father, Jean Marie Charles Le Bon, was forty-one and a minor functionary of the French government. Both parents were of solid French middle-class stock; their Breton and Bourguignon ancestry can be traced back several hundred years. Gustave Le Bon was a direct descendant of Jean-Odet Carnot, 1645–1726, whose granddaughter, Claudine Carnot, married Louis Le Bon, a French government functionary, in 1761. Jean-Odet's grandfather, Jean Carnot, who died in 1626, had a brother Denys from whom President Sadi Carnot of the French Third Republic was directly descended.

When Gustave was eight years old, his father was transferred to a new post and the family, including Gustave's younger brother Georges, left Nogent-le-Rotrou never to return. Nevertheless, the town is proud that Gustave Le Bon was born there and named a street after him.

Little is known about Gustave's childhood except that he was graduated from a lycée at Tours where he was not an outstanding student. In 1860, he went on to the University of Paris and then pursued medical studies at the Faculty of Medicine. He served his internship at Hôtel Dieu hospital in Paris and completed his medical studies in 1866. From then on, he called himself "Doctor" though he never went into formal medical practice as a physician.

Le Bon's school and university years were a kind of compulsory apprenticeship for his own self-development. His first published writing, which appeared in 1862, dealt with the illnesses of people living in swampy areas. He next wrote several articles about calabar fever and asphyxiation. His first full-length book, published in 1866, showed at once that he was far ahead of his time and that he would have been intellectually more at home in scientific America a century later. Entitled *Apparent Death and Premature Burials,* the book concerned a subject featured in today's newspaper headlines—the definition of death.

When is a person "dead"? Le Bon tried to find the answers. He claimed and proved that many patients were presumed to be dead who in fact were not. He recommended life-sustaining or restoring techniques which then were regarded as weird or useless but which are now adapted and perfected as a matter of common practice. Naturally, Le Bon's book offended the panjandrums of medicine in France. How dare this young man argue about who was dead and who wasn't? Dead is dead, everyone knew that, and especially all medical doctors knew it. Only, it seems they didn't always know. Now in the 1970s, top-ranking members of the medical profession argue several of the same questions about death which that arrogant nineteenth-century upstart, Gustave Le Bon, had raised.

His voracious interest in science impelled him toward physiological and anthropological studies. He recorded his observations in nontechnical terms so that any reader could understand the text. In 1868, he wrote a textbook about reproduction of the species in man and animals. Eleven editions were sold out within two years. Again Le Bon irritated the academic hierarchy. Abhorring genteelisms, he graphically explained the scientific sexual and physiological information he deemed essential for better understanding of life, human physiology, and history.

When the Franco-Prussian War began, Le Bon, then living in Paris, volunteered for medical service. He organized a division of military ambulances and served as its doctor-in-chief. In that capacity, he observed and reflected on the behavior of the military under the worst possible condition—total defeat. Equipped with a first-hand knowledge of warfare, of military discipline, and of the behavior of men under conditions of utmost stress and suffering, he wrote tracts on military leadership that were admired and partly heeded by the ablest generals in the French army and were studied at St. Cyr and other military academies in France and abroad. At the end of the war, Le Bon was named a Chevalier of the Legion of Honor.

Then came the Paris Commune of 1871, which he witnessed, and which was in some ways worse than the Reign of Terror (1793–94). Gustave Le Bon, then thirty years old, watched as the Parisian revolutionary crowds burned the beautiful palace of the Tuileries, the library of the Louvre, the Renaissance City Hall and

Theater, the tapestry factory of Gobelins, part of the Palace of Justice, the home of the Legion of Honor, and other irreplaceable works of architectural art.

From 1871 to 1914, Le Bon persistently attacked the socialist pacifists and antimilitarists who, he believed, were gravely weakening France. Having seen war and Prussian military might coupled with remarkable German powers of organization and industrialization, Le Bon strove to strengthen France and to enhance her military prestige and ability. Therefore he remained aloof from the Dreyfus Affair which divided Frenchmen into two irreconcilable factions. He avoided the political adventurism of General Georges Boulanger. In 1913, Le Bon's *Aphorisms of Present Times* was published. Under the heading "Pacifism and War," he wrote:

> If nature had not been pitiless toward the weak, the world would be peopled by monsters, and no civilization would have dawned.
>
> The only people having the right to be pacifist are those armed with lots of cannons.
>
> To withdraw in face of an effort believed to be useless is to renounce in advance all success.
>
> Fear of being defeated augments the chances of being defeated.

Concerning revolution, Le Bon wrote:

> The really unhappy one is he who can be persuaded that his condition is miserable. It is on this basis that leaders proceed to make revolutions.

Mental contagion is the most powerful factor in the propagation of a revolutionary movement.

In certain men, the revolutionary spirit is a mental condition independent of the object on which it is exercised. No concession could appease them.

Every popular revolution which succeeds is a momentary return to barbarism. The revolution constitutes the triumph of instinct over rationality, the rejection of social constraints that differentiate the civilized individual from the barbarian.

Great social reforms are not the work of revolutions. These operate, as in geological upheavals, through a slow accumulation of little causes.

The immediate result of a revolution is generally but a shift in servitude.

Although the world today recognizes Le Bon's *The Psychology of the Crowd* as an immortal contribution to knowledge, his book *Opinions and Beliefs,* published in 1911, is an equally great or perhaps still greater *chef d'oeuvre* in social psychology. Written after he had abandoned his laboratory research in physics in 1908, the work reflects his ability to draw on the scientific knowledge he so arduously acquired, and on its inspiration, to return to his study of psychology in a more masterful, more profound and all-encompassing way.

How did it happen that a *chef d'oeuvre* by a philosopher already world famous because of an acknowledged masterwork, *The Psychology of the Crowd,* was ignored or permitted to slip into obscurity? It seems that *Opinions and Beliefs,* even more than *The Psychology of*

Socialism published thirteen years earlier, offended the "devotees" of socialism. Far more accurately and profoundly than the British author George Orwell later portrayed in his brilliant novel *1984,* Le Bon predicted in *Opinions and Beliefs* that the destruction of individual liberty and degradation of civilization would come through socialism, syndicalism, and communism, and that Marxism would replace Christianity and other religions. Also, he insisted that psychology is a science, and that psychological understanding is essential to the study of sociology and history.[9]

Dedicated to his friend Gabriel Hanotaux, former French Minister of Foreign Affairs, with the inscription "To that eminent historian whose penetrating wisdom knows how to discover visible facts under the weft of invisible forces that determine them," *Opinions and Beliefs* opens with the flat statement:

> The problem of belief, sometimes confused with that of knowledge, is nevertheless strongly distinct from it. To know and to believe are different things not having the same genesis.
> From opinions and beliefs derive our concepts of life, our conduct, and consequently most of the happenings of

---

[9] In a conversation with Alice Widener concerning Gustave Le Bon, March 1978, President Raymond Polin, University of Sorbonne-Paris, said: "Also, Le Bon's works offended his eminent French contemporary, the sociologist Émile Durkheim, who would not admit that psychology has anything to do with sociology and conducted a veritable war against Le Bon."

history. They are governed, like all phenomena, by certain rules, but these rules are not yet determined.

Le Bon goes on to explain that even Blaise Pascal, the great seventeenth-century French philosopher, refrained from trying to ascertain the rules, saying that if he did not deal with it, the reason was that he felt himself so incapable and inadequate that he came to believe the task impossible of accomplishment.

Aware of the insuperable difficulties, Le Bon modestly but resolutely decided to try his best to ascertain the rules governing beliefs. "Thanks to modern scientific discoveries," he wrote, "it seems possible for us to approach the problem before which Pascal drew back."

Le Bon said that the problem of beliefs had haunted him ever since he first studied history, for it seemed to him that human belief is its principal factor. Because Descartes had described belief as rational and voluntary, Le Bon said, most subsequent authors had accepted the interpretation. Le Bon opened his *Opinions and Beliefs* with the statement, "One of the objectives of this book is to show that belief is neither voluntary nor rational." He continued:

How can one explain the extraordinary fact that beliefs determine the creation and fall of powerful civilizations? Nomad tribes, lost in the depths of Arabia, adopt a religion that a single inspired leader teaches them, and thereupon found within less than fifty years an empire as vast as that of Alexander's, an empire illustrated by a splendid display of marvelous monuments.

A few centuries earlier, semibarbarian people are converted to a faith preached by some apostles from an
obscure corner of Galilee and under the regenerating fires
of belief, the old world crumbles and gives way to a new
and different civilization in which every element remains
impregnated with the memory of a God to which it had
given birth.

Almost twenty centuries later, the old faith is shaken,
unknown stars appear in the skies of thought, and a people
arise who pretend to be able to break all ties to the past.
Their destructive but powerful faith, despite the anarchy
into which this great Revolution plunges them, has the
strength necessary to dominate Europe by force of arms
and to make a victorious march across all its capitals.

The problem of the establishment and propagation of
opinions, and above all of beliefs, has aspects so marvelous, said Le Bon, that the sects of each religion invoke its creation and diffusion as proof of divine origin.
These aspects lead to the observation that beliefs are
adopted despite their being contrary to the most evident
self-interest of those who accept them. For example,
Le Bon asked, how can the secret force be explained
that led a Roman legionnaire or consul to despoil himself of his worldly goods and risk frightful tortures to
adopt a new religion contrary to established customs,
disdained by reason and forbidden by law? Thus, it is
impossible to attribute intellectual weakness to the men
who voluntarily submitted themselves to such bondage
to belief, from antiquity to present times, since the
same phenomena are observed among the most cultivated minds.

To Le Bon, a theory to be valid must help explain why the most illustrious scholars, renowned for their critical minds, accept legends so childishly naive as to be laughable from any rational, scientific point of view. Hence, to explain belief, it is necessary to define it and to show how it is distinct from knowledge, for, he wrote:

> A belief is an act of faith of unconscious origin which forces us to admit as an entity an idea, an opinion, an explanation, a doctrine. Reason is foreign to its formation. By the time a belief tries to justify itself, it is already formed. Everything that is accepted by a simple act of faith must be qualified as a belief. If its exactitude is later verified by observation and experience, it ceases to be a belief and becomes knowledge.

Proceeding from this analysis, Le Bon argued that belief and knowledge constitute two modes of distinctly different mental activity of very different origin: an unconscious intuition engendered by causes independent of our will, and a conscious acquisition edified by exclusively rational methods, such as experience and observation.

It was only at an advanced stage of history, he explained, that humanity, submerged in the world of belief, discovered the world of knowledge. In penetrating it, all the phenomena heretofore attributed to the will of superior beings were unfolded as being subject to the influence of inflexible laws.

Owing solely to the fact that men were approaching

the outskirts of knowledge, he said, all former concepts of the universe were changed. But in this new sphere, it was not yet possible to penetrate very far. The progress of science reveals each day, said Le Bon, that its discoveries remain impregnated by the unknown. The most precise realities are shrouded by mysteries. Science is full of such shadows and behind the horizon it has attained, others appear, lost in the infinite which seems ever to recede.

"A mystery," wrote Le Bon, "is the unknown soul of things."

Opinions and Beliefs lies untranslated and neglected partly because it runs counter to socialism, the dominant belief of our age, the belief described by Le Bon as a revolution of people pretending to sever all ties with the past,[10] the revolution now triumphantly marching across all capitals in the world. Le Bon said:

> The great domain which no philosophy has been able to illuminate is the kingdom of dreams. They are replete with hopes which no reasoning will be able to destroy. Therein all religious, political and other kinds of beliefs find limitless power. The unconquerable phantoms who inhabit it are created by faith.
>
> To know and to believe always will remain different. Though the acquisition of even the smallest scientific truth

---

[10] Perhaps the clearest, shortest expression of the revolutionist's wish to break all ties with the past was uttered by British pro-Communist film producer John Grierson who, in October 1945, wrote in *Film News* that educators should get rid of all static past concepts, such as "the tattered friezes of the Parthenon."

demands an enormous labor, the possession of a certitude having faith alone as its support requires none at all. All men possess beliefs; very few are able to lift themselves up to knowledge.

Noting that the world of belief possesses its own logic and laws which scholars have tried in vain to penetrate with their own methods, Le Bon insisted that in *Opinions and Beliefs* "one will see why the scholar loses all critical spirit in penetrating the cycle of belief and meets therein only the most deceptive illusions."

Knowledge, said Le Bon, is an essential element of civilization and is the main factor of its material progress. Belief orients the thoughts and opinions of a civilization and, as a result, its conduct.

Once thought to be of divine origin, he explained, beliefs were accepted without discussion. We know today that beliefs emanate from within ourselves. Yet they nevertheless impose themselves upon us. Reason has in general as little effect on beliefs as on hunger or thirst. Elaborated in subconscious areas which intelligence cannot reach, a belief is undergone and is not discussable. The unconscious and therefore involuntary nature of beliefs renders them very strong. Whether religious, political or social, said Le Bon, they always play a preponderant role in history.

Beliefs, become generalized, constitute the attractive poles around which people's existence gravitates, said Le Bon, and put their stamp on all the elements of a civilization. The Buddhist civilization, the Muslim civilization and Christian civilization are correct appellations, "but in becoming the center of attraction, belief also becomes the center of deformation. The diverse elements of social life—philosophy, the arts and literature—modify themselves in order to adapt to it."

According to Le Bon, the only real revolutions are those which renew the fundamental beliefs of a people.

> Such revolutions have been very rare in history. It is in name only that a conviction transforms itself. Faith changes its central object but never dies. Faith cannot die because the need to believe constitutes an ineluctable psychological element as irreducible as pleasure and pain. The human soul has a horror of doubt and uncertainty. Man sometimes traverses phases of skepticism but cannot dwell there. He needs to be guided by a religious, political or moral *credo* which dominates him and avoids for him the effort of thinking. Dogmas that are destroyed always are replaced.
>
> On such indestructible necessities reason has no hold.

He asserted that our modern age is as much affected by faith as that of any preceding one.

> Dogmas as despotic as those of the past are preached in the new temples in which there can be counted as many faithful as in the old. The old religious credos that enslaved the crowd are replaced by socialist or anarchist credos just as imperious and unreasonable but nonetheless dominating people's souls. The church may be replaced by the sports arena or cabaret, but the sermons preached by mystical leaders are heard and received with the same faith.

Without doubt, faith in any dogma is generally nothing but an illusion. Nevertheless, one must not disdain it. Thanks to its magical power, the unreal becomes more potent than the real. An accepted faith gives to people a community of thought generating their unity and force.

Noting that the domain of knowledge is very different from that of belief, he argued that it is useless to oppose one to the other. Science, disengaged more and more from belief, remains nevertheless very heavily permeated by it. Science is subjected to belief in all poorly known fields—the mysteries of life or the origin of the species, for example. The theories that are accepted are simple articles of faith enjoying only the authority of the masters who formulate them.

The laws controlling the psychology of belief are applicable not only to the great fundamental convictions which left an indelible stamp on the course of history, but also to most of our daily opinions on the beings and things which surround us.

Observation shows easily that the majority of these opinions, Le Bon said, are supported not by rational elements, but by affective or mystical ones generally of an unconscious nature.

If one sees them discussed with such ardor, it is precisely because they arise from the domain of beliefs and are formed in the same way. Frequently distinct in their effects, beliefs and opinions nevertheless belong to the same family, though knowledge belongs to a completely different world.

Nowhere in all his works did Gustave Le Bon, the man, reveal himself more clearly than in his *Opinions and Beliefs:*

> I thought about all this for years under different skies. Sometimes it was while contemplating those thousands of statues raised during eighty centuries to the glory of the gods incarnating our dreams. Sometimes it was while I was amid the gigantic pillars of strange architectural temples reflected in the majestic waters of the Nile or built on the tormented banks of the Ganges. How could one admire those marvels without thinking of the secret forces that made them emerge from a void in which no rational thought would have caused them to arise? . . . Knowledge and belief—that is the whole of our civilization and history.

Immediately following *Opinions and Beliefs,* Gustave Le Bon wrote *The Psychology of Revolutions,* published in 1912. Besides offending socialists and communists by pointing out the fatuousness of trying to solve human problems through the class struggle, he attacked the most fundamental of all revolutionists' beliefs—the concept of the perfectibility of man. "Human nature," declared Le Bon, "must be accepted as it is."

Though he analyzed several revolutions, he paid most attention to the French Revolution of 1789–93 in which theorists tried for the first time in history "to transform man and society in the name of reason." They had power greater than that of any despot, and yet "despite this power, despite the success of the armies, despite Draconian laws and repeated *coups d'état,* the Revolution merely heaped ruin upon ruin, and ended in dictatorship." However, such an attempt was not totally useless, he argued, because experience is necessary to education and because the French people did gain certain rights not previously enjoyed. But these probably would have been obtained in a much less sanguinary and evolutionary way, he said, as consequences of future scientific and technological progress. Moreover, he said, "Without the Revolution, it would have been difficult to prove that pure reason does not enable us to change human nature and, consequently, that no society can be rebuilt by the will of legislators, however absolute their power."

Le Bon's argument that society cannot be rebuilt by legislators is anathema not only to all socialists and communists but also to all democratic utopians.

> Action is always hurtful when, despising realities, it professes violently to change the course of events. One cannot experiment with society as with apparatus in a laboratory.

At the end of *The Psychology of Revolutions,* Le Bon warned of a world war resulting from the Germans' mystical belief in themselves as a master race and the Prussian belief in militarism as the best means to world hegemony: "In the center of Europe, a formidable military power is increasing in strength, and is aspiring to dominate the world in order to find outlets for its goods and for an increasing population. . . ."

He warned his fellow countrymen in France against

the weakening effects of their political party rivalries, base religious prejudices, socialist pacifism, and most of all their retarding of French industrial progress through enactment of highly restrictive, regulatory laws.

In June 1914, former President Theodore Roosevelt of the United States, deeply troubled over the threat of war in Europe, went there to try to find out for himself what was the real situation. He had written to former French Minister of Foreign Affairs Gabriel Hanotaux asking him to gather together a group of outstanding French thinkers who might furnish an insight into the political, military, and economic state of things. Roosevelt specifically requested that Dr. Gustave Le Bon be invited. Of the occasion, Le Bon wrote:

> During the luncheon, the late President was both brilliant and profound. His steady and exact reasoning brought him quickly to the heart of every question.
>
> After speaking of the part which ideas play in the guidance of all great national leaders, Roosevelt, fixing his penetrating gaze upon me, said in a grave voice, "There is a little book which has never left me in all my travels and which was always to be found on my table during my presidency. This book is your *Psychological Laws of the Evolution of Peoples.*
>
> The President then explained at length the instruction which, according to him, this book contained.

President Roosevelt was not the only political leader instructed by Le Bon's "little book" written in 1894 and soon translated into Japanese by Baron Motono,

Japan's minister of foreign affairs, and also translated into Turkish and Arabic. Tragically, Roosevelt was one of the very few Western statesmen who studied Le Bon's *Psychological Laws of the Evolution of Peoples.* However, a young Russian who went to Paris in 1895 well schooled in Karl Marx studied it. His name was Vladimir Ilyich Ulyanov, later and better known as Nikolai Lenin. In 1917, as leader of the Bolsheviks, Lenin overthrew the freely elected Constituent Assembly in Russia and became dictator of the Union of Soviet Socialist Republics. Thereafter, Le Bon's book was on Lenin's work table, with passages heavily marked and underlined. Later, the "little book" was studied by Benito Mussolini and Adolf Hitler. But most intellectuals of the West shunned or ignored Le Bon's great work, though it was what they sorely needed for understanding the psychological forces at work in the real world.

Except for a very few independent-minded leaders such as Theodore Roosevelt, only the destined dictators in our century studied profoundly the works of Gustave Le Bon. The dictators put his great psychological discoveries to misuse while almost all so-called defenders of what Le Bon so eloquently described as "the glory and the charm of our civilization" left his discoveries in disuse.

As Dr. John R. Pierce, the famous American scientist, says, "That which Le Bon observed so clearly is powerfully at work in the world."

Edited Extracts
from the Major Works of
Gustave Le Bon

Prefatory Note

The process of choosing what the selector believes to be the best in the works of Gustave Le Bon, a prolific writer whose professional career spanned seventy years, cannot be objective. No two readers could agree on what is best. To try to avoid purely subjective personal preference, I have sought to excerpt from Le Bon's outstanding works in chronological order those passages which seem to be most pertinent to our present times and of greatest possible interest to contemporary scholars and students.

Gustave Le Bon wrote a preface and introduction to almost all his works. It also was his practice to write a new introduction to a major reprinting of one of his works, thus affording himself the opportunity to restate, correct, or amplify his previous ideas. All emphasis in the selections is his.

Part I

Psychological Laws of the Evolution of Peoples

(Lois Psychologiques de l'Évolution des Peuples)

First edition published in Paris by F. Alcan, 1894. First published in English in the United States by G. E. Stechert, New York, 1924, and reprinted from that edition by Arno Press, New York, 1974.

Introduction
(twelfth edition, 1927)

The life of peoples is controlled by a small number of invariable psychological factors. These function throughout time and space, everywhere and always. From the banks of the Ganges to the plains of Europe, they contribute forcefully to the birth and decline of the greatest empires. . . .

The psychological forces . . . are not born of reason and dominate all reason. It is only in books that one sees rationality guiding history.

General Conclusions
(first edition)

A race possesses psychological characteristics almost as fixed as its physical characteristics. Like anatomic species, the psychological species transforms itself only very slowly.

To the fixed and hereditary psychological character-istics, the association of which forms the mental constitution of a race, are added, as in all anatomic species, accessory elements created by diverse modifications of environment. Ceaselessly renewed, they endow a race with an apparent extended variability.

The mental constitution of a race represents not only the synthesis of the living beings who compose it, but above all, that of the numerous ancestors who contributed toward forming it. It is not the living but the dead who play the preponderant role in the existence of a people. They constitute the creators of its morale and the unconscious drive of its conduct.

The very great anatomic differences which distinguish the various human races are accompanied by psychological differences no less considerable. When one compares only the average representatives of each people, the mental differences often seem rather slight. These become immense as soon as the comparison relates to the most elevated elements of the peoples. One then establishes that what differentiates the superior from the inferior races is above all that the former possess a certain number of highly developed intellects while the latter do not.

Individuals composing inferior races present a manifest equality among themselves. In proportion as races elevate themselves on the ladder of civilization, their members tend more and more to become differentiated. The inevitable effect of civilization is to differentiate individuals and races. It is therefore not toward equality that peoples are progressing but toward a growing inequality.

The life of a people and all the manifestations of its civilization are the simple reflection of its soul, the visible signs of an invisible but very real thing. Exterior events are merely the apparent surface of the hidden web that determines them.

It is not chance or exterior circumstances nor above all political institutions that play the fundamental role in the history of a people. It is above all its character.

The various elements of the civilization of a people being but exterior symptoms of its mental constitution, the expression of certain ways of feeling and of thinking peculiar to that people cannot be transmitted unchanged to peoples of a different mental constitution. The only elements that can be transmitted are exterior and superficial forms without importance.

The profound differences that separate the mental constitution of various peoples result in making them perceive the outside world in very dissimilar ways. The result is that they feel, reason and act in very different ways and consequently find themselves in disagreement on all questions as soon as they come into contact. Most of the wars that fill history were born of these disagreements. Wars of conquest, wars of religion, wars of dynasties have always been in reality wars of races.

An agglomeration of men of different origins succeeds in forming a race, that is, in possessing a collective soul, only when, after repeated interbreeding during centuries and a similar existence under identical surroundings, they have acquired common sentiments, common interests and common beliefs.

Among civilized peoples there are almost no natural races, but only artificial ones created by historic conditions.

Changes of environment profoundly influence only new races, that is to say, those mixtures of ancient races whose ancestral character has been dissociated by crossbreeding. Heredity alone is powerful enough to struggle against heredity. Upon races whose crossings did not succeed in destroying their character, changes of environment have only a purely destructive action. An ancient race perishes rather than submit to transformations necessitating adaptation to new environment.

The acquisition of a solidly constructed collective soul marks the apogee of a people's greatness. Its dissociation marks the hour of its decadence. The intervention of foreign elements represents one of the surest means of arriving at such disassociations.

The psychological species submit, as do the anatomic species, to the effects of time. They are equally condemned to grow old and to fade away. Always very slow in forming themselves, they can, on the contrary, disappear rapidly. It suffices to disturb profoundly the functioning of their organs to make them submit to regressive transformations of which the result often is a very prompt destruction. Peoples require long centuries to acquire a certain mental constitution and sometimes lose it in a very short time.

Next to character, one must place ideas as one of the principal factors in the evolution of a civilization. They do not act until, after a slow evolution, they are transformed into sentiments and consequently form a part of character. They escape then the influence of reasoning and require a very long time to disappear. Every civilization is derived from a small number of fundamental ideas universally accepted.

Among the most important guiding ideas of a civilization are its religious ideas. The majority of historical events have emerged indirectly from the variation of religious beliefs. The history of humanity is parallel to that of its gods. The birth of new gods has always marked the dawn of a new civilization. These progeny of our dreams have such power that their very name cannot be changed without immediately overturning the world.

Part II

The Crowd

(Psychologie des Foules)

First edition published in Paris by F. Alcan, 1895. First published in English in the United States by the Macmillan Company (original firm no longer in existence), New York, 1896; republished by Viking Press, New York, 1960; paperback edition by Viking Press, 1969.

Preface

Organized crowds always have played an important part in the life of peoples, but this part never has been of such moment as at present. The substitution of the unconscious action of crowds for the conscious activity of individuals is one of the principal characteristics of the present age.

Introduction

The present epoch is one of those critical moments in which the thought of mankind is undergoing a process of transformation. Two fundamental factors are at the base of this transformation. The first is the destruction of those religious, political and social beliefs in which all the elements of our civilization are rooted. The second is the creation of entirely new conditions of existence and thought as the result of modern scientific and industrial discoveries.

The ideas of the past, although half destroyed, being still very powerful, and the ideas which are to replace them being still in process of formation, the modern age represents a period of transition and anarchy. . . .

While all our ancient beliefs are tottering and disappearing, while the old pillars of society are giving way one by one, the power of the crowd is the only force that nothing menaces, and of which the prestige is continually on the increase. The age we are about to enter will in truth be the *era of crowds.*

The Mind of Crowds

In its ordinary sense the word "crowd" means a gathering of individuals of whatever nationality, profession, or sex, and whatever be the chances that have brought them together. From the psychological point of view, the expression "crowd" assumes quite a different significance. Under certain given circumstances, and only under those circumstances, an agglomeration of men presents new characteristics very different from those of the individuals composing it. The sentiments and ideas of all the persons in the gathering take one and the same direction, and their conscious personality vanishes. A collective mind is formed, doubtless transitory, but presenting very clearly defined characteristics. The gathering has thus become what, in the absence of a better expression, I will call an organized crowd, or, if the term is considered preferable, a psychological crowd. It forms a single being and is subject to the *law of the mental unity of crowds.*

It is not by the mere fact of a number of individuals finding themselves accidentally side by side that they acquire the character of an organized crowd. A thousand individuals accidentally gathered in a public place without any determined objective in no way constitute a crowd from the psychological point of view. To acquire the special characteristics of such a crowd, the influence of certain predisposing causes is necessary. . . .

Thousands of isolated individuals may acquire at certain moments, and under the influence of certain violent emotions—such, for example, as a great national event—the characteristics of a psychological crowd. . . . At certain moments, half a dozen men might constitute a psychological crowd. . . . On the other hand, an entire nation, though there may be no visible agglomeration, may become a crowd under the action of certain influences. . . .

The most striking peculiarity presented by a psychological crowd is the following: Whatever be the individuals who compose it, however like or unlike be their mode of life, their occupations, their character or their intelligence, the fact that they have been transformed into a crowd puts them in possession of a sort of collective mind which makes them feel, think and act in a manner quite different from that in which each individual among them would feel, think and act were he in a state of isolation. There are certain ideas and

feelings which do not come into being, or do not trans-
late themselves into acts except in the case of individuals forming a crowd. The psychological crowd is a
provisional being formed of heterogeneous elements
which for a moment are combined. . . .

In the aggregate which constitutes a crowd there is
in no way a summing-up of or an average struck between its elements. What really takes place is a combi-
nation followed by the creation of new characteristics,
just as in chemistry certain elements, when brought into
contact . . . combine to form a new body possessing
properties quite different from those of the bodies that
served to form it.

In the collective mind the intellectual aptitudes of
the individuals, and in consequence their individuality,
are weakened. The heterogeneous is swamped by the
homogeneous, and the unconscious qualities obtain the
upper hand.

This very fact that crowds possess in common ordinary qualities explains why they can never accomplish
acts demanding a high degree of intelligence. . . . The
truth is, they can only bring to bear in common on the
work in hand those mediocre qualities which are the
birthright of every average individual. . . .

If the individuals of a crowd confined themselves to
putting in common the ordinary qualities of which
each of them has his share, there would merely result
the striking of an average and not . . . the creation of

new characteristics. How is it that these new characteristics are created?

Different causes determine the appearance of characteristics peculiar to crowds that are not possessed by individuals. The first is that the individual forming part of a crowd acquires solely from numerical considerations a sentiment of invincible power allowing him to yield to instincts which, had he been alone, he would perforce have kept under restraint. He will be the less disposed to check himself from the consideration that, a crowd being anonymous and in consequence irresponsible, the sentiment of responsibility which always controls individuals disappears entirely.

The second cause is contagion, which also intervenes to determine in crowds the manifestation of their special characteristics and the trend they will take. Contagion is a phenomenon easy to establish the presence of, but not easy to explain. It must be classed among those phenomena of a hypnotic order. . . . In a crowd every sentiment and act is contagious, and contagious to such a degree that an individual readily sacrifices his personal interest to the collective interest. This is an aptitude very contrary to his nature, and of which a man is scarcely capable except when he makes part of a crowd.

A third cause . . . is suggestibility, of which, moreover, contagion is neither more nor less than an effect.

The most careful observations seem to prove that

an individual immerged for some length of time in a crowd in action soon finds himself—either in consequence of the magnetic influence given out by the crowd, or from some other cause of which we are ignorant—in a special state much resembling the state of fascination in which the hypnotized individual finds himself in the hands of the hypnotizer. . . . The conscious personality has entirely vanished: will and discernment are lost. All feelings and thoughts are bent in the direction determined by the hypnotizer. . . .

The individual forming part of a psychological crowd . . . is no longer conscious of his acts. In his case . . . certain faculties are destroyed, others may be brought to a high degree of exaltation. Under the influence of a suggestion, he will undertake the accomplishment of certain acts with irresistible impetuosity. . . . The individualities in the crowd who might possess a personality sufficiently strong to resist the suggestion are too few in number to struggle against the current. At the utmost, they may be able to attempt a diversion by means of different suggestions. It is in this way . . . that a happy expression, an image opportunely evoked, has occasionally deterred crowds from the most bloodthirsty acts. . . .

By the mere fact that he forms part of an organized crowd, a man descends several rungs in the ladder of civilization. Isolated, he may be a cultivated individual; in a crowd, he is a barbarian—that is, a creature acting by instinct. He possesses the spontaneity, the violence, the ferocity, and also the enthusiasm and heroism of primitive beings, whom he further tends to resemble by the facility with which he allows himself to be impressed by words and images—which would be entirely without action on each of the isolated individuals composing the crowds—and to be induced to common acts contrary to his most obvious interests and his best-known habits. An individual in a crowd is a grain of sand amid grains of sand which the wind stirs up at will.

It is for these reasons that juries are seen to deliver verdicts of which each individual juror would disapprove, that parliamentary assemblies adopt laws and measures of which each of their members would disapprove in his own person. Taken separately, the men of the French Revolutionary Convention were enlightened citizens of peaceful habits. United in a crowd, they did not hesitate to give their consent to the most savage proposals, to guillotine individuals most clearly innocent and, contrary to their interests, to renounce their inviolability and to decimate themselves.

It is not only by his acts that the individual in a crowd differs essentially from himself. Even before he has entirely lost his independence, his ideas and feelings have undergone a transformation, and the transformation is so profound as to change the miser into a spendthrift, the skeptic into a believer, the honest man into a criminal, and the coward into a hero. . . .

The conclusion to be drawn . . . is that the crowd is always intellectually inferior to the isolated individual, but . . . from the point of view of feelings and of the acts these feelings provoke, the crowd may, according to circumstances, be better or worse than the individual. All depends on the nature of the suggestion to which the crowd is exposed. This is the point that has been completely misunderstood by writers who have studied crowds from only the criminal point of view.

It is crowds rather than isolated individuals that may be induced to run the risk of death to secure the triumph of a creed or an idea, that may be fired with enthusiasm for glory and honor, that are led on—almost without bread and without arms, as in the age of the Crusades—to deliver the tomb of Christ from the infidel, or, as in [17] '93, to defend the [French] fatherland.

Concerning the faculty of observation possessed by the crowd, our conclusion is that their collective observations are as erroneous as possible, and that most often they merely represent the illusion of an individual who, by a process of contagion, has influenced his fellows. . . . Thousands of men were present . . . at the celebrated cavalry charge during the battle of Sedan, and yet it is impossible, in the face of the most contradictory eye-witness testimony, to decide by whom it was commanded. The English general, Lord Wolseley, has proved . . . that up to now the gravest errors of fact have been committed with regard to the most important incidents of the battle of Waterloo—facts that hundreds of witnesses had nevertheless attested. . . .

Had not the past left us its literary and artistic works and monuments, we should know absolutely nothing in reality with regard to bygone times. Are we in possession of a single word of truth concerning the lives of the great men who played such preponderant parts in the history of humanity—men such as Hercules, Buddha, or Muhammad? In all probability we are not. In point of fact, moreover, their real lives are of slight importance to us. Our interest is to know what our great men were as they are presented by popular legend. It is legendary heroes, and not for a moment real heroes, who have impressed the minds of crowds.

Unfortunately, legends . . . have in themselves no stability. The imagination of the crowd continually transforms them as the result of the lapse of time, and especially in consequence of racial causes. There is a great gulf fixed between the sanguinary Jehovah of the Old Testament and the God of Love of Saint Theresa, and the Buddha worshipped in China has no traits in common with that venerated in India.

It is not even necessary that heroes should be separated from us by centuries for their legend to be transformed by the imagination of the crowd. . . . In our own day we have seen the legend of the greatest heroes modified several times in less than fifty years. Under the Bourbons, Napoleon became a sort of idyllic and liberal philanthropist, a friend of the humble who, according to the poets, was destined to be long remembered in the [peasant] cottage. Thirty years afterward, this easygoing hero had become a sanguinary despot who, after having usurped power and destroyed liberty, caused the slaughter of three million men solely to satisfy his ambition. At present we are witnessing a fresh transformation of the legend. . . . When it has undergone the influence of some dozens of centuries, the learned men of the future, face to face with these contradictory accounts, will perhaps doubt the very existence of the hero, as some now doubt that of Buddha, and will see in him nothing more than a solar myth or a development of the legend of Hercules. . . . They will doubtless console themselves easily for this uncertainty, for, better initiated than we are today in the characteristics and psychology of crowds, they will know that history is scarcely capable of preserving the memory of anything except myths.

The Intolerance, Dictatorship, and Conservatism of Crowds

Crowds are cognizant only of simple and extreme sentiments; the opinions, ideas and beliefs suggested to them are accepted or rejected as a whole, and considered as absolute truths or as no less absolute errors. This always is the case with beliefs induced by a process of suggestion instead of engendered by reasoning. . . .

A crowd is always ready to revolt against a feeble and to bow down servilely before a strong authority. Should the strength of an authority be intermittent, the crowd, always obedient to its extreme sentiments, passes alternately from anarchy to servitude, and from servitude to anarchy.

However, to believe in the predominance among crowds of revolutionary instincts would be to misconstrue entirely their psychology. It is merely their tendency to violence that deceives us on this point. Their rebellious and destructive outbursts are always very transitory. Crowds are too much governed by unconscious considerations, and too much subject in consequence to secular hereditary influences not to be extremely conservative. Abandoned to themselves, they soon weary of disorder, and instinctively turn to servitude. . . .

It is difficult to understand history, and popular revolutions in particular, if one does not take sufficiently into account the profoundly conservative instincts of crowds. They may be desirous, it is true, of changing the names of their institutions, and to obtain these changes they accomplish at times even violent revolutions, but the essence of these institutions is too much the expression of hereditary needs of the race for them not to abide by it invariably. . . . Their fetish-like respect for all traditions is absolute; their unconscious horror of all novelty capable of changing the essential conditions of their existence is very deeply rooted.

The Morality of Crowds

Taking the word "morality" to mean constant respect for certain social conventions, and the permanent repression of selfish impulses, it is quite evident that crowds are too impulsive and too mobile to be moral. If, however, we include in the term morality the transitory display of certain qualities such as abnegation, self-sacrifice, disinterestedness, devotion, and the need of equity, we may say on the contrary that crowds may exhibit at times a very lofty moralism. . . .

How numerous are the crowds that have heroically faced death for beliefs, ideas, and phrases that they scarcely understood! The crowds that go on strike do so far more in obedience to an order than to obtain an increase of the meager wages with which they make shift. Personal interest is very rarely a powerful motive force with crowds, while it is almost the exclusive motive of the conduct of the isolated individual. It is assuredly not self-interest that has guided crowds in so many wars, incomprehensible as a rule to their intelligence—wars in which they have allowed themselves to be massacred as easily as larks hypnotized by the mirror of a hunter.

If disinterestedness, resignation and absolute devotion to a real or chimerical ideal are moral virtues, it may be said that crowds often possess these virtues to a degree rarely attained by the wisest philosophers. . . . We should not complain too much that crowds are more especially guided by unconscious considerations and are not given to reasoning. In certain cases, had they reasoned and consulted their immediate interests, it is possible that no civilization could have grown up on our planet, and humanity would have had no history.

The Ideas, Reasoning, Power, and Imagination of Crowds

Such ideas as are accessible to crowds . . . may be divided into two classes. In one we shall place accidental and passing ideas created by the influences of the moment; infatuation for an individual or a doctrine, for instance. In the other will be classed the fundamental ideas, to which the environment, the laws of heredity, and public opinion give a very great stability; such ideas are the religious beliefs of the past and the social and democratic ideas of today. . . .

Whatever be the ideas suggested to crowds, they can only exercise effective influence on condition that they assume a very absolute, uncompromising and simple shape. They present themselves in the guise of images, and are only accessible to the masses under this form. These image-like ideas are not connected by any logical bond of analogy or succession, and may take each other's place like the slides of a magic lantern. . . .

A long time is necessary for ideas to establish themselves in the minds of crowds, but just as long a time is needed for them to be eradicated. For this reason crowds, as far as ideas are concerned, are always several generations behind learned men and philosophers. All statesmen are well aware today of the admixture of error contained in the [crowd's] fundamental ideas

. . . but are obliged to govern in accordance with principles in the truth of which they have ceased to believe. . . .

The mode of reasoning of crowds resembles that of the Eskimo who, knowing from experience that ice, a transparent body, melts in the mouth, concludes that glass, also a transparent body, should also melt in the mouth; or that of the savage who imagines that by eating the heart of a courageous foe he acquires his bravery; or of the workman who, having been exploited by one employer, immediately concludes that all employers exploit their men.

The characteristics of the reasoning of crowds are the association of dissimilar things possessing a merely apparent connection . . . and the immediate generalization of particular cases. It is arguments of this kind that are always presented to crowds by those who know how to manipulate them. An orator in intimate communication with a crowd can evoke images by which it will be seduced. . . .

The powerlessness of crowds to reason aright prevents their displaying any trace of the critical spirit, prevents their . . . being capable of discerning truth from error, or of forming a precise judgment in any matter. . . .

Crowds, being capable of thinking only in images, are impressed only by images. It is only images that terrify or attract them and become motives of action. . . . It was not by means of cunning rhetoric that

Antony succeeded in making the populace rise against the murderers of Caesar; it was by reading his will to the multitude and pointing to his corpse. . . .

The power of conquerors and the strength of states is based on the popular imagination. . . . All great historical facts, the rise of Buddhism, of Christianity, of Islam, the Reformation, the French Revolution, and, in our own times, the threatening invasion of socialism are the direct or indirect consequences of strong impressions produced on the imagination of the crowd.

The Convictions of Crowds

The crowd always demands a god before everything else. . . . Were it possible to induce the masses to adopt atheism, this belief would exhibit all the intolerant ardor of a religious sentiment, and in its exterior forms would soon become a cult.

The Opinions and Beliefs of Crowds

The factors which determine the opinions and beliefs [of crowds] are of two kinds: remote factors and immediate factors.

The remote factors are those which render crowds capable of adopting certain convictions and absolutely refractory to the acceptance of others. These factors prepare the ground in which are suddenly seen to germinate certain new ideas whose force and consequences are a cause of astonishment, though they are spontaneous only in appearance. The outburst and putting into practice of certain ideas among crowds presents at times a startling suddenness. This is only a superficial effect behind which must be sought a preliminary and preparatory action of long duration.

The immediate factors are those which, coming on top of this long preparatory working . . . serve as the source of active persuasion on crowds; that is, they are the factors causing the idea to take shape and setting it loose with all its consequences. . . .

Among the remote facts there are some of a general nature, which are found to underlie all the beliefs and opinions of crowds. These are race, traditions, time, institutions, and education. . . .

Race must be placed in the first rank, for in itself it far surpasses in importance all others. . . . Environment, circumstances and events represent the social suggestions of the moment. They may have a considerable influence, but this influence always is momentary if it be contrary to the suggestions of the race; that is, to those which are inherited by a nation from the entire series of its ancestors. . . .

Traditions represent the ideas, the needs, and the sentiments of the past. They are the synthesis of the race and weigh upon us with immense force. . . . Civilization is impossible without traditions, and progress is impossible without the destruction of those traditions. The difficulty, and it is an immense one, is to find a proper equilibrium between stability and variability. . . .

In social as in biological problems, time is . . . the sole creator and the sole great destroyer. . . .

Dependent on it [the influence of time on the genesis of the opinions of crowds] are the great forces such as race, which cannot form themselves without it. . . . It is time in particular that prepares the opinions and beliefs of crowds, or at least the soil on which they will germinate. This is why certain ideas are realizable at one epoch and not at another. . . .

The idea that institutions can remedy the defects of societies, that national progress is the consequence of the improvement of institutions and governments, and that social changes can be effected by decrees . . . is still generally accepted. . . . The most continuous experience has been unsuccessful in shaking this grave delusion. . . . A nation does not choose its institutions at will any more than it chooses the color of its hair or its eyes. Institutions and governments are the product of the race. . . . Institutions have no intrinsic virtue; in themselves they are neither good nor bad. Those which are good at a given moment for a given people may be harmful in the extreme for another nation. . . . Moreover, it is in no way in the power of a people really to change its institutions. Undoubtedly, at the cost of violent revolutions, it [a people] can change their name, but in their essence they [the institutions] are unmodified. . . .

Peoples are governed by their character, and all institutions not intimately modeled on that character merely represent a borrowed garment, a transitory disguise. . . . It is illusion and words that have influenced the mind of the crowd, and especially words—words which are as powerful as they are chimerical.

Images, Words, and Formulas

The power of words is bound up with the images they evoke, and is quite independent of their real significance. Words whose sense is the most ill-defined are sometimes those that possess the most influence. Such, for example, are the terms democratic, socialism, equality, liberty, etc., whose meaning is so vague that thick volumes do not suffice to fix it precisely. . . .

Reason and arguments are incapable of combating certain words and formulas. They are uttered with solemnity in the presence of crowds, and as soon as they have been pronounced an expression of respect is visible on every countenance and all heads are bowed. . . .

The images evoked by words being independent of their sense, they vary from age to age and from people to people, the formulas remaining identical. . . .

Words, then, have only mobile and transitory significance which change from age to age and people to people; and when we desire to exert an influence by their means on the crowd, it is necessary to know the meaning given them by the crowd at a given moment and not that which they formerly had or may yet have for individuals of a different mental constitution.

Thus, when crowds have come, as the result of political upheavals or changes of belief, to acquire a profound antipathy for the images evoked by certain words, the first duty of the true statesman is to change the words without, of course, laying hands on the things themselves. . . . One of the most essential functions of statesmen consists, then, in baptizing with popular or at any rate indifferent words things the crowd cannot endure under their old names. The power of words is so great that it suffices to designate in well-chosen terms the most odious things to make them acceptable to crowds. . . . Taine justly observes that it was by invoking liberty and fraternity—words very popular at the time—that the Jacobins were able "to instill a despotism worthy of Dahomey, a tribunal similar to that of the Inquisition, and to accomplish human hetacombs akin to those of ancient Mexico." The art of those who govern, as is the case with the art of advocates, consists above all in the science of employing words.

Illusions

From the dawn of civilization onward, crowds always have undergone the influence of illusions. It is to the creators of illusions that they have raised more temples, statues and altars than to any other class of men. . . .

The philosophers of the last century [eighteenth] devoted themselves with fervor to the destruction of the religious, political and social illusions on which our forefathers had lived for a long sequence of centuries. By destroying them they dried up the springs of hope and resignation. Behind the immolated chimeras, they came face to face with the blind and silent forces of nature which are inexorable toward weakness and ignore pity. . . . Not truth but error has always been the chief factor in the evolution of nations, and the reason why socialism is so powerful today is that it constitutes the last illusion that still is vital.

Experience

Experience constitutes almost the only effective process by which a truth may be solidly established in the mind of the masses, and illusions grown too dangerous destroyed. To this end, however, it is necessary that the experience should take place on a very large scale, and be very frequently repeated. The experiences undergone by one generation are useless, as a rule, for the generation that follows, which is the reason why historical facts cited with a view to demonstration serve no purpose. . . .

To prove to us experimentally that dictators cost the nations who acclaim them dear, two ruinous experiences have been sufficiently convincing. . . . To bring an entire nation to admit that the huge German army was not, as was currently alleged thirty years ago, a sort of harmless national guard, the terrible war [1870] which cost us [France] so dear had to take place. To bring about the recognition that [tariff] protection ruins the nations which adopt it, at least twenty years of disastrous experience will be needed. These examples might be indefinitely multiplied.

Reason

In enumerating the factors capable of making an impression on the minds of crowds, all mention of reason might be dispensed with were it not necessary to point out the negative value of its influence. . . .

It is not even necessary to descend so low as primitive beings to obtain an insight into the utter powerlessness of reasoning when it has to fight against sentiment. Let us merely call to mind how tenacious, for centuries long, have been religious superstitions in contradiction with the simplest logic. . . .

Should it be regretted that crowds never are guided by reason? We should not venture to affirm it. Without a doubt human reason would not have availed to spur humanity along the path of civilization with the ardor and hardihood its illusions have done.

Let us leave reason, then, to philosophers, and not insist too strongly on its intervention in the governing of men. It is not by reason, but most often in spite of it, that are created those sentiments which are the mainsprings of all civilization—sentiments such as honor, self-sacrifice, religious faith, patriotism, and the love of glory.

The Leaders of Crowds

As soon as a certain number of living beings are gathered together, whether they be animals or men, they place themselves instinctively under the authority of a chief. In the case of human crowds, the chief is often nothing more than a ringleader or agitator, but as such he plays a considerable part. His will is the nucleus around which the opinions of the crowd are grouped and attain identity. . . . A crowd is a servile flock incapable of ever doing without a master.

The leader has most often started as one of the led. He himself has been hypnotized by one idea, whose apostle he has since become. . . . The multitude is always ready to listen to the strong-willed man, who knows how to impose himself upon it. Men gathered in a crowd lose all force of will, and turn instinctively to the person possessing the quality they lack.

Nations never have lacked leaders, but all of the latter have by no means been animated by those strong convictions proper to apostles. . . .

In every social sphere, from the highest to the lowest, as soon as a man ceases to be isolated he speedily falls under the influence of a leader. The majority of men, especially among the masses, do not possess clear and reasoned ideas on any subject whatsoever outside their own specialty. The leader serves them as guide. . . .

The leaders of crowds wield a very despotic authority, and this despotism is indeed a condition of their obtaining a following. It has often been remarked how easily they extort obedience, although without any means of backing up their authority, from the most turbulent sections of the working classes. They fix the hours of labor and the rate of wages, and they decree strikes which are begun and ended at the hour they ordain. . . .

The Means of Action of Leaders: Affirmation, Repetition, Contagion

When it is wanted to stir up a crowd for a short space of time to induce it to commit an act of any nature—to pillage a palace, or to die in defense of a stronghold or a barricade, for instance—the crowd must be acted upon by rapid suggestions among which example is the most powerful in effect. To attain this end, however, it is necessary that the crowd should have been previously prepared by certain circumstances and above all, that he who wishes to work upon it should possess . . . prestige.

When, however, it is proposed to imbue the mind of a crowd with ideas and beliefs—with modern social theories, for instance—the leaders have recourse to different expedients. The principal ones are three in number and clearly defined—affirmation, repetition and contagion. . . .

Affirmation, pure and simple, kept free of all reasoning and all proof, is one of the surest means of making an idea enter the mind of crowds. The more concise and more destitute of every appearance of proof and demonstration, the more weight affirmation carries. . . .

Affirmation, however, has no real influence unless it be constantly repeated, and so far as possible in the same terms. . . .

The influence of repetition on crowds is comprehensible when the power that it exercises on the most enlightened minds is seen. This power is due to the fact that the repeated statement is embedded in the long run in those profound regions of our unconscious selves to which the motives of our actions are forged. At the end of a certain time we have forgotten who is the author of the repeated assertion, and we finish by believing it. To this circumstance is due the astonishing power of advertising. . . .

When an affirmation has been sufficiently repeated and there is unanimity in this repetition . . . what is called a current of opinion is formed and the powerful mechanism of contagion intervenes. Ideas, sentiments, emotions and beliefs possess in crowds a contagious power as intense as that of microbes. . . .

For individuals to succumb to contagion their simultaneous presence on the same spot is not indispensable. The action of contagion may be felt from a distance under the influence of events giving all minds an individual trend and the characteristics peculiar to crowds. . . .

Imitation, to which so much influence is attributed in social phenomena, is in reality a mere effect of contagion. . . .

Prestige

Whatever has been a ruling power in the world, whether it be ideas or men, has in the main enforced its authority by means of that irresistible force expressed by the word "prestige." . . . Prestige may involve such sentiments as admiration or fear . . . but it can perfectly well exist without them. The greatest measure of prestige is possessed by the dead. . . .

Prestige, in reality, is a sort of domination exercised on our minds by an individual, a work, or an idea. This domination entirely paralyzes our critical faculty and fills our soul with admiration and respect. . . . Prestige is the mainspring of all authority. Neither gods, kings nor women have ever reigned without it.

The various kinds of prestige may be grouped under two principal heads: acquired prestige and personal prestige. Acquired prestige is that resulting from name, fortune and reputation. . . . Personal prestige, on the contrary, is something essentially peculiar to the individual; it may coexist with reputation, glory and fortune, or be strengthened by them, but it is perfectly capable of existing in their absence. . . .

Personal prestige . . . is a faculty independent of all titles, of all authority, and possessed by a small number of persons whom it enables to exercise a veritably magnetic fascination on those around them, although they are socially their equals, and lack all ordinary means of domination. They force the acceptance of their ideas and sentiments on those about them, and they are obeyed as is the tamer of wild beasts by the animal that could easily devour him.

The great leaders of crowds, such as Buddha, Jesus, Muhammad, Joan of Arc, and Napoleon, have possessed this form of prestige in a high degree, and to this endowment is more particularly due the position they attained. Gods, heroes and dogmas win their way in the world from their own inward strength. . . .

The great personages I have just cited were in possession of their power of fascination long before they became illustrious, and would never have become so without it. . . .

Prestige lost by want of success disappears in a brief space of time. It can also be worn away, but more slowly, by being subjected to discussion. . . . From the moment prestige is called into question, it ceases to be prestige. The gods and men who have kept their prestige for long have never tolerated discussion. For the crowd to be admiring, it must be kept at a distance.

Limitations of the Variability of the Beliefs and Opinions of Crowds

A close parallel exists between the anatomical and psychological characteristics of living beings. . . .

The same phenomenon is observed in the case of

moral characteristics. Alongside the unalterable psychological elements of a race, mobile and changeable elements are to be encountered. For this reason, in studying the beliefs and opinions of a people, the presence is always detected of a fixed groundwork on which are engrafted opinions as changing as the surface sand on a rock.

The opinions and beliefs of crowds may be divided . . . into two very distinct classes. On the one hand we have great permanent beliefs, which endure for several centuries, and on which an entire civilization may rest. Such, for instance, in the past were feudalism, Christianity, and Protestantism; and such, in our own time, are the nationalist principle and contemporary democratic and social ideas. In the second place there are the transitory changing opinions, the outcome as a rule of general conceptions of which every age sees the birth and disappearance; examples . . . are the theories which mold literature and the arts—those, for instance, which produced romanticism, naturalism, mysticism, etc. Opinions of this order are, as a rule, as superficial as fashion and as changeable. . . .

The great generalized beliefs are very restricted in number. Their rise and fall form the culminating points of the history of every human race. They constitute the real framework of civilization.

It is easy to imbue the mind of crowds with a passing opinion, but very difficult to implant therein a lasting belief. However, a belief of this latter description once established is equally difficult to uproot. Usually it is to be changed only at the cost of violent revolutions. Even revolutions can avail only when the belief has almost entirely lost its sway over men's minds. In that case, revolutions serve finally to sweep away what had already been almost cast aside, though the force of habit prevented its complete abandonment. The beginning of a revolution is in reality the end of a belief.

The precise moment at which a great belief is doomed is easily recognizable: it is the moment when its value begins to be called in question. Every general belief being little else than a fiction, it can survive only on condition that it not be subjected to examination. But even when a belief is severely shaken, the institutions to which it has given rise retain their strength and disappear but slowly. Finally, when the belief has completely lost its force, all that rested upon it soon is involved in ruin. As yet a nation never has been able to change its beliefs without being condemned at the same time to transform all the elements of its civilization. . . . General beliefs are the indispensable pillars of civilizations; they determine the trend of ideas. They alone are capable of inspiring faith and creating a sense of duty. . . .

As soon as a new dogma is implanted in the mind of crowds it becomes the source of inspiration from which are evolved its institutions, arts, and mode of existence.

Thanks to general beliefs, the men of every age are enveloped in a network of traditions, opinions and customs which render them all alike and from whose yoke they cannot extricate themselves. . . . The tyranny exercised unconsciously on men's minds is the only real tyranny because it cannot be fought against. Tiberius, Genghis Khan and Napoleon were assuredly redoubtable tyrants, but from the depth of their graves Moses, Buddha, Jesus and Muhammad have exerted on the human soul a far profounder despotism. In its violent struggle with Roman Catholicism, it is the French Revolution that has been vanquished, and this despite the fact that the sympathy of the crowd was apparently on its side, and despite recourse to destructive measures as pitiless as those of the Inquisition. The only real tyrants that humanity has known always have been the memories of its dead or the illusions it has forged for itself.

The philosophic absurdity that often marks general beliefs has never been an obstacle to their triumph . . . In consequence, the evident weakness of the socialist beliefs of today will not prevent their triumph among the masses. . . . The socialist ideal of happiness being intended to be realized on earth [instead of only in a future life, as in all other religions], the vanity of its promises will at once appear as soon as the first efforts toward their realization are made, and simultaneously the new belief will lose its prestige entirely. Its strength, therefore, will only increase until the day when, having triumphed, its practical realization will commence. For this reason, while the new religion, like all those which have preceded it, begins by exerting a destructive influence, it will be unable in the future to play a creative role.

The Changeable Opinions of Crowds

At the present time the changeable opinions of crowds are greater in number than ever before, and for three different reasons:

The first is that as the old beliefs are losing their influence to a greater and greater extent, they are ceasing to shape the ephemeral opinions of the moment as they did in the past. The weakening of general beliefs clears the ground for a crop of haphazard opinions without a past or future.

The second reason is that the power of crowds being on the increase, and this power being less and less counterbalanced, the extreme mobility of ideas, which we have seen to be a peculiarity of crowds, can manifest itself without let or hindrance.

Finally, the third reason is the recent development of the newspaper press, by whose agency the most contrary opinions are being continually brought before the attention of crowds. The suggestions that might result from each individual opinion are soon destroyed by suggestions of an opposite character. The consequence is that no opinion succeeds in becoming widespread, and that the existence of all of them is ephemeral. . . . Nothing is more mobile and changeable than the thought of crowds, and nothing more frequent than to see them execrate today what they applauded yesterday.

The total absence of any sort of direction of opinion, and at the same time the destruction of general beliefs, have had for final result an extreme divergency of convictions of every order, and a growing indifference on the part of crowds to everything that does not plainly touch their immediate interests. . . .

The man of modern times is more and more a prey to indifference. . . .

A civilization, when the moment has come for crowds to acquire a high hand over it, is at the mercy of too many chances to endure for long. Could anything postpone for a while the hour of its ruin, it would be precisely the extreme instability of the opinions of crowds and their growing indifference and lack of respect for all general beliefs.

The Classification of Crowds

We will, first of all, set forth in a few words the general classification of crowds.

Our starting point will be the simple multitude. Its most inferior form is . . . when the multitude is composed of individuals belonging to different races. In this case its only common bond of union is the will, more or less respected, of a chief. The barbarians of very diverse origin who during several centuries invaded the Roman Empire may be cited as a specimen of the multitudes of this kind.

On a higher level . . . are those [multitudes] which under certain circumstances have acquired common characteristics, and have ended by forming a single race. . . .

These two kinds of multitudes may, under certain influences, . . . be transformed into organized or psychological crowds. We shall break up these organized crowds into the following divisions:

A. Heterogeneous crowds	1. Anonymous crowds (street crowds, for example).
	2. Crowds not anonymous (juries, parliamentary assemblies, etc.).
B. Homogeneous crowds	1. Sects (political sects, religious sects, etc.).
	2. Castes (the military caste, the priestly caste, the working caste, etc.).
	3. Classes (the middle classes, the peasant classes, etc.).

Heterogeneous Crowds

These collectivities [heterogeneous crowds] . . . are composed of individuals of any description, of any profession, and any degree of intelligence. . . .

A fundamental factor, that of race, allows of a toler-

ably thorough differentiation of the various heterogeneous crowds. . . .

A crowd composed of individuals assembled at haphazard, but all of them Englishmen or Chinese, will
differ widely from another crowd also composed of
individuals of any and every description, but of other
races—Russians, Frenchmen, or Spaniards, for example.

The wide divergencies which their inherited mental
constitution creates in men's modes of feeling and
thinking come at once into prominence when, which
rarely happens, circumstances gather together in the
same crowd and in fairly equal proportions individuals
of different nationalities, and this occurs, however identical in appearance be the interests which provoked the
gathering. The efforts made by the socialists to assemble in great congresses the representatives of the working class populations of different countries always have
ended in the most pronounced discord. A Latin crowd,
however revolutionary or however conservative it is
supposed to be, will invariably appeal to the intervention of the state to realize its demands. It is always
distinguished by a marked tendency toward centralization and by a leaning, more or less pronounced, in
favor of a dictatorship. An English or American crowd,
on the contrary, sets no store on the state and only
appeals to private initiative. A French crowd lays particular stress on equality and an English crowd on
liberty. These differences of race explain how it is that

there are almost as many different forms of socialism and democracy as there are nations.

The genius of the race, then, exerts a paramount influence upon the disposition of a crowd. . . . It should be considered as an essential law that *the inferior characteristics of crowds are the less accentuated in proportion as the spirit of the race is strong.* The crowd state with the domination of crowds is equivalent to the barbarian state, or to a return to it. It is by acquisition of a solidly constituted collective spirit that the race frees itself to a greater and greater extent from the unreflecting power or crowds and emerges from the barbarian state.

Homogeneous Crowds

Homogeneous crowds include: 1. Sects; 2. Castes; 3. Classes.

The *sect* represents the first step in the process of organization of homogeneous crowds. A sect includes individuals differing greatly as to their education, professions, and the class of society to which they belong and with their common beliefs as the connecting link. Examples . . . are religious and political sects.

The *caste* represents the highest degree of organization of which the crowd is susceptible. . . . The caste is composed of individuals of the same profession and in consequence similarly educated and of much the same social status. Examples . . . are the military and priestly castes.

The *class* is formed of individuals of diverse origin . . . linked together by certain interests and certain habits of life and education almost identical. The middle class and agricultural class are examples.

Crowds Termed Criminal Crowds

Owing to the fact that crowds, after a period of excitement, enter upon a purely automatic and unconscious state, in which they are guided by suggestion, it seems difficult to qualify them in any case as criminal. I only retain this erroneous qualification because it has been brought into definite vogue by recent psychological investigations. . . .

The usual motive of the crimes of crowds is a powerful suggestion, and the individuals taking part in such crimes are afterwards convinced that they have acted in obedience to duty, which is far from being the case with the ordinary criminal. . . .

The general characteristics of criminal crowds are precisely the same as . . . in all crowds: openness to suggestion, credulity; mobility; the exaggeration of good or bad sentiments; the manifestation of certain forms of morality, etc.

Juries in Criminal Cases

Being unable to study here every category of jury, I shall examine only the most important—that of the juries of the French Court of Assize. These juries afford an excellent example of the heterogeneous crowd that is not anonymous. We shall find them displaying suggestibility and but slight capacity for reasoning, while they are open to the influence of the leaders of crowds, and they are guided in the main by unconscious sentiments. . . .

At the present time, jurors are recruited for the most part from among small tradesmen, petty capitalists and employees. Yet, to the great astonishment of informed writers, whatever the composition of the jury has been, its decisions have been identical. Like all crowds, juries are very strongly impressed by sentimental considerations and very slightly by argument. . . . Without pity for crimes of which it appears possible they might themselves be victims—such crimes, moreover, are the most dangerous for society—juries are, on the contrary, very indulgent in the case of breaches of the law whose motive is passion. . . .

Juries, like all crowds, are profoundly impressed by prestige, and M. [Bernard] des Glajeux [a former President of the Court of Assize] very properly remarks that, though very democratic as juries are in their composition, they are very aristocratic in their likes and dislikes: "Name, birth, great wealth, celebrity, the assistance of an illustrious counsel, everything in the nature of distinction or that lends brilliancy to the accused, stands him in extremely good stead.". . .

We should cling vigorously to the jury. It constitutes, perhaps, the only category of crowd that cannot be replaced by any individuality. It alone can temper the severity of the law, which, equal for all, in principle ought to be blind and to take no cognizance of particular cases. Inaccessible to pity and heeding nothing but the text of the law, the judge in his professional capacity would visit the same penalty on the burglar guilty of murder and the wretched girl whom poverty and her abandonment by her seducer have driven to infanticide. The jury, on the other hand, instinctively feels that the seduced girl is much less guilty than the seducer, who, however, is not touched by the laws, and that she deserves every indulgence. . . .

I do not perceive a single case in which, wrongly accused of a crime, I should not prefer to have to deal with a jury rather than with magistrates. . . . The power of crowds is to be dreaded, but the power of certain castes is to be dreaded even more. Crowds are open to convictions, castes never are.

Electoral Crowds

Electoral crowds—that is to say, collectivities invested with the power of electing the holders of certain functions—constitute heterogeneous crowds. . . .

The psychology of electoral crowds . . . is identical with that of other crowds: neither better nor worse. . . . The dogma of universal suffrage possesses today the power that the Christian dogma formerly possessed. Orators and writers allude to it with respect and adulation that never fell to the share of Louis XIV. In consequence the same position must be taken with regard to it as to all religious dogmas. Time alone can act upon them. . . . Must it be believed that with a suffrage restricted to those intellectually capable, if it be desired, an improvement would be effected in the votes of crowds? I cannot admit for a moment that this would be the case, . . . for the reasons that I have already given concerning the mental inferiority of all collectivities, whatever their composition. In a crowd, men always tend to the same level and, on general questions, a vote cast by forty academicians is no better than that of forty water-carriers. . . .

It does not follow because an individual knows Greek or mathematics, is an architect, a veterinary surgeon, doctor or barrister, that he is endowed with a special intelligence on social questions. All our political economists are highly educated, being for the most part professors or academicians, yet is there a single general question—protection, bimetallism, etc.—on which they have succeeded in agreeing? The explanation is that their science is only a very attenuated form of our universal ignorance. With regard to social problems, owing to the number of unknown quantities they offer, men are, substantially, equally ignorant. . . .

In each country, the average opinions of those elected represent the genius of the race, and they will be found not to alter sensibly from one generation to another. . . . Peoples are guided in the main by the genius of their race, that is, by that inherited residue of qualities of which the genius is the sum total. Race and the slavery of our daily necessities are the mysterious master-causes that rule our destiny.

Parliamentary Assemblies

In parliamentary assemblies we have an example of heterogeneous crowds that are not anonymous. Although the mode of election of their members varies from epoch to epoch, and from nation to nation, they present very similar characteristics. In this case, the influence of the race makes itself felt to weaken or exaggerate the characteristics common to crowds, but not to prevent their manifestation. . . .

The parliamentary system represents the ideal of all modern civilized peoples. The system is the expression of the idea, psychologically erroneous, but generally subscribed to, that a large gathering of men is much more capable than a small number of coming to a wise and independent decision on a given subject. . . .

Men forming a crowd cannot do without a master, whence it results that the votes of an assembly only represent, as a rule, the opinions of a small minority. . . . The influence of the leaders is due in very small measure to the arguments they employ, but in a large degree to their prestige. . . .

A leader is seldom in advance of public opinion; almost always all he does is follow it and espouse all its errors. . . .

On occasion, the leader may be intelligent and highly educated, but the possession of these qualities does him, as a rule, more harm than good. By showing how complex things are, by allowing of explanation and promoting comprehension, intelligence always renders its owner indulgent and blunts in large measure that intensity and violence of conviction necessary to apostles. The great leaders of crowds of all ages, and those of the [French] Revolution in particular, have been of lamentably narrow intellect, while it is precisely those whose intelligence has been the most restricted who have exercised the greatest influence.

The speeches of the most celebrated of them, of Robespierre, frequently astound one by their incoherence; by merely reading them no plausible explanation is to be found for the great part played by the powerful dictator. . . .

It is terrible . . . to think of the power that strong conviction combined with extreme narrowness of mind gives a man possessing prestige. . . .

In a parliamentary assembly the success of a speech depends almost solely on the prestige possessed by the speaker, and not at all on the arguments he brings forward. The best proof of this is that when for one reason or another a speaker loses his prestige, he loses simultaneously all his influence, that is, his power of influencing votes at will. . . .

When parliamentary assemblies reach a certain pitch of excitement they become identical with ordinary heterogeneous crowds, and their sentiments in consequence present the peculiarity of being always extreme. They will be seen to commit acts of the greatest heroism or the worst excess. The individual is no longer himself, and so entirely is this the case that he will vote measures most adverse to his personal interests. . . .

Fortunately, all the characteristics . . . met with in parliamentary assemblies are in no wise constantly displayed. Such assemblies only constitute crowds at certain moments. The individuals composing them retain their individuality in a great number of cases, which explains how it is that an assembly is able to turn out excellent technical laws. It is true that the author of these laws is a specialist who has prepared them in the quiet of his study, and that in reality the law voted is the work of an individual and not of an assembly. These laws are naturally the best. They are only liable to have disastrous results when a series of amendments has converted them into the outcome of a collective effort. The work of the crowd always is inferior, whatever its nature, to that of an isolated individual. It is specialists who safeguard assemblies from passing ill-advised or unworkable measures. The specialist in this case is a temporary leader of crowds. The assembly is without influence on him, but he has influence over the assembly.

In spite of all the difficulties attending their functioning, parliamentary assemblies are the best form of government mankind has discovered as yet, and more especially the best means it has found to escape the yoke of personal tyrannies. . . .

Moreover, in reality they present only two serious dangers, one being inevitable financial waste, and the other the progressive restriction of the liberty of the individual.

The first of these dangers is the necessary consequence of the exigencies and want of foresight of electoral crowds. Should a member of an assembly propose a measure giving apparent satisfaction to democratic ideas, should he bring in a bill, for instance, to assure old-age pensions to all workers and to increase the wages of any class of state employees, the other deputies, victims of suggestion in their dread of the electors, will not venture to seem to disregard the interests of the latter by rejecting the proposed measures, although well aware that they are imposing a fresh strain on the budget and necessitating the creation of new taxes. . . .

In addition to this first cause of an exaggerated expenditure, there is another not less imperative—the necessity of voting all grants for local purposes. A deputy is unable to oppose grants of this kind because they represent . . . the exigencies of the electors and because each individual deputy can only obtain what he requires for his own constituency on the condition of acceding to similar demands on the part of his colleagues. . . .

The second of the dangers referred to—the inevitable restrictions on liberty imposed by parliamentary assemblies—is . . . less obvious but nevertheless very real. It is the result of the innumerable laws—always having a restrictive action—which parliaments consider themselves obliged to vote, and to whose consequences, owing to their shortsightedness, they are in a great measure blind. . . .

Herbert Spencer has shown . . . that the increase of apparent liberty must be followed by the decrease of real liberty. . . .

The progressive restriction of liberties shows itself in every country in a special form which Herbert Spencer has not pointed out; it is that the passing of these innumerable series of legislative measures, all of them in a general way of a restrictive order, serves necessarily to augment the number, power and influence of the functionaries charged with their application. These functionaries tend in this way to become the veritable masters of civilized countries. Their power is all the greater owing to the fact that, amidst the incessant transfer of authority, the administrative caste is alone in possessing irresponsibility, impersonality and perpetuity. There is no more oppressive despotism than that which presents itself under this triple form. . . .

This incessant creation of restrictive laws and regulations, surrounding the pettiest actions of existence with the most complicated formalities, inevitably has for its result the confining within narrower and narrower limits the sphere in which the citizen may move freely. Victims of the delusion that equality and liberty are the better assured by the multiplication of laws, nations daily consent to put up with increasingly burdensome trammels. . . .

Arrived at this point, the individual is bound to seek outside himself the forces he no longer finds within himself. The functions of governments necessarily increase in proportion as the indifference and helplessness of the citizens grow. . . . The state becomes an all powerful god. . . .

This progressive restriction of all liberties in the case of certain peoples, in spite of an outward license giving them the illusion that these liberties are still in their possession, seems at least as much a consequence of their old age as of any particular system. It constitutes one of the precursory symptoms of that decadent phase which up to now no civilization has escaped. Judging by the lessons of the past, and by the symptoms that strike one's attention on every side, several of our modern civilizations have reached that phase of old age which precedes decadence. . . .

It is easy to note briefly these common phases of the evolution of civilizations, and I shall end this work with a summary of them. This rapid sketch will perhaps throw some gleams of light on the causes of the power at present wielded by crowds.

If we examine in their main lines the genesis of the greatness and fall of civilizations that preceded our own, what do we see?

At the dawn of civilization a horde of men of various origins are brought together by chances of migrations, invasions and conquests. Of different blood, and of equally different languages and beliefs, the only common bond of union among these men is the half-recognized law of a chief. The psychological characteristics of crowds are present in an eminent degree in these confused agglomerations. They have the transient cohesion of crowds, their heroism, their weaknesses, their impulsiveness and their violence. Nothing is stable in connection with them. They are barbarians.

At length time accomplishes its work. The identity of surroundings, the repeated intermingling of races, the necessities of life in common exert their influence. The assemblage of dissimilar units begins to blend into a whole, to form a race, an aggregate possessing common characteristics and sentiments to which heredity will give greater and greater fixity. The crowd has become a people, and this people is able to emerge from its barbarous state. However, it will emerge therefrom entirely only when it shall have acquired an ideal. The nature of this ideal is of slight importance, whether it be the cult of Rome, the might of Athens, or the triumph of Allah; it will suffice to endow all the individuals of the race being formed with perfect unity of sentiment and thought.

At this state a new civilization, with its institutions, its beliefs and its arts may be born. In pursuit of its ideal, the race will acquire in succession the qualities necessary to give it splendor, vigor and grandeur. At times . . . it will still be a crowd, but henceforth, beneath the mobile and changing characteristics of crowds, is found a solid substratum, the genius of the race which confines within narrow limits the transformations of a nation and overrules the play of chance.

After having exerted its creative action, time begins that work of destruction from which neither gods nor men escape. Having reached a certain level of strength and complexity, a civilization ceases to grow, and having ceased to grow it is condemned to a speedy decline. The hour of its old age has struck. This inevitable hour always is marked by the weakening of the ideal that was the mainstay of the race. In proportion as this ideal pales, all the religious, political and social structures inspired by it begin to be shaken.

With the progressive perishing of its ideal, the race loses more and more qualities that lent it cohesion, its unity and its strength. The personality and intelligence of the individual may increase, but at the same time his collective egoism of the race is replaced by an excessive development of the ego of the individual, accompanied by a weakening of character and a lessening of the capacity for action. What constituted a people, a unity, a whole, becomes in the end an agglomeration of individualities lacking cohesion and artificially held together for a time by its traditions and institutions. It is at this stage that men, divided by their interests and aspirations, and incapable any longer of self-government, require direction in their pettiest acts, and that the state exerts an absorbing influence.

With the definite loss of its old ideal, the genius of the race disappears entirely; it is a mere swarm of isolated individuals and returns to its original state, that of a crowd. Without consistency and without a future, it has all the transitory characteristics of crowds. Its civilization is now without stability and at the mercy of every chance. The populace is sovereign, and the tide of barbarism mounts. The civilization may still seem brilliant because it possesses an outward front, the work of a long past, but it is in reality an edifice crumbling to ruin, which nothing supports, and is destined to cave in at the first storm.

To pass in pursuit of an ideal from the barbarous to the civilized state, and then, when the ideal has lost its virtue, to decline and die, such is the cycle of the life of a people.

Part III

The Psychology
of Socialism

(Psychologie du Socialisme)

First edition published in Paris by F. Alcan, 1898. First published in English in the United States by the Macmillan Company, New York, 1899; reprinted by the Fraser Publishing Company, Wells, Vermont, 1965.

No apostle has ever doubted the future of his faith, and the socialists are persuaded of the approaching triumph of theirs. Such a victory implies of necessity the destruction of the present society, and its reconstruction on other bases. To the disciples of the new dogmas, nothing appears more simple. . . . But does our modern knowledge of the evolution of things allow us to admit that man is able to refashion according to his liking a society that has been so destroyed?

As soon as we penetrate a little into the mechanism of civilizations, we quickly discover that a society, with its institutions, its beliefs, and its arts, represents a tissue of ideas, sentiments, customs and modes of thought determined by heredity, the cohesion of which constitutes its strength. No society is firmly held together unless this moral heritage is solidly established, and established not in codes but in the natures of men; the one declines when the other crumbles, and when this moral heritage is finally disintegrated, the society is doomed to disappear. . . .

Thanks to its promise of regeneration, thanks to the hope it flashes before all the disinherited of life, socialism is becoming a belief of a religious character rather than a doctrine. Now the great power of beliefs, when they tend to assume this religious form . . . lies in the fact that their propagation is independent of the proportion of truth or error that they may contain, for as soon as a belief has gained a lodging in the minds of men, its absurdity no longer appears; reason cannot reach it, and only time can impair it.

Socialism, whose dream is to substitute itself for the ancient faiths, proposes only a very low ideal, and to establish it appeals to sentiments lower still. . . . With what lever does it seek to raise the soul? With the sentiments of envy and hatred which it creates in the hearts of the multitudes. To the crowd, no longer satisfied with political and civic equality, it proposes equality of condition, without dreaming that social inequalities are born of those natural inequalities that man has always been powerless to change.

The Various Aspects of Socialism

What in effect is socialism, speaking philosophically —or, at least, what is its best-known form, collectivism? Simply a reaction of the collective being against the encroachments of individual beings. Now if we put aside the interests of intelligence, and the possibly immense utility of husbanding these interests for the progress of civilization, it is undeniable that the collectivity—if only by that law of the greater number which has become the great *credo* of modern democracies—may be considered as invented to subject to itself the individual sprung from its loins, and who would be nothing without it. For centuries, that is to say during the succession of the ages which have preceded our own, the collectivity has always been all-powerful, at least among the Latin peoples. The individual outside it was nothing. Perhaps the French Revolution, the culmination of all the doctrines of the eighteenth-century writers, represents the first serious attempt at reaction by individualism, but in enfranchising the individual (at least theoretically), it has also isolated him. In isolating him from his caste, from his family, from the social or religious groups of which he was a unit, it has left him delivered over to himself, and has thus transformed society into a mass of individuals without cohesion and without ties.

Such a work cannot have very lasting results. Only the strong can support isolation and rely only on themselves: the weak are unable to do so. To isolation, and the absence of support, they prefer servitude; even painful servitude. The castes and corporations destroyed by the revolution formed of old the fabric which served to support the individual in life; and it is evident that they corresponded to a psychological necessity, since they are reviving on every hand under various names today, and notably under that of trade-unions. These associations permit the individual to reduce his efforts to a minimum, while individualism obliges him to increase his efforts to the maximum. Isolated, the proletarian is nothing and can do nothing; incorporated he becomes a redoubtable force. If incorporation is unable to give him capacity and intelligence, it does at least give him strength, and forbids him nothing but a liberty he wouldn't know what to do with.

From the philosophic point of view, then, socialism is certainly a reaction of the collectivity against the individual—a return to the past. Individualism and collectivism are, in their general essentials, two opposing forces which tend, if not to annihilate, at least to paralyze one another. In this struggle between the generally conflicting interests of the individual and those of the aggregate lies the true philosophic problem of socialism. The individual who is sufficiently strong to count only on his own intelligence and initiative, and is therefore highly capable of making headway, finds himself face to face with the masses, feeble in initiative and intelligence, but to whom their number gives might, the only upholder of right. The interests of the two opposing parties are conflicting. The problem is to discover whether they can maintain themselves without destroying themselves, at the price of reciprocal concessions. Hitherto, religion has succeeded in persuading the individual to sacrifice his personal interests to those of his fellows only to replace individual egoism by the collective egoism. But the old religions are in sight of death, and those that must replace them are yet unborn. In investigating the evolution of the social solidarity, we have to consider how far conciliation between the two contradictory principles is allowed by economic necessities. . . .

To complete our examination of the various aspects of socialism we must consider its variations in respect to race. . . . Among the vigorous and energetic races which have arrived at the culminating point of their development, we observe a considerable extension of what is confided to personal initiative, and a progressive reduction of all that is left to the state to perform; and this is true of republics equally with monarchies. We find a precisely opposite part given to the state by those peoples among whom the individual has arrived at such a degree of mental exhaustion as no longer permits him to rely on his own forces. For such peoples, whatever may be the names of their institutions, the government is always a power absorbing everything, manufacturing everything, and controlling the smallest details of the citizen's life. Socialism is only the extension of this concept. It would be a dictatorship —impersonal but absolute.

The Origin of Socialism

Socialism has not made its first appearance in the world today. . . . We may say that . . . its prime cause is the inequality of conditions, and this inequality was the law of the ancient world as it is that of the modern. Unless some all-powerful deity takes it upon himself to remodel the nature of man, this inequality is undoubtedly destined to subsist until the final sterilization of our planet. It would seem that the struggle between rich and poor must be eternal.

Without harking back to primitive communism, a form of inferior development from which all societies have sprung, we may say that antiquity has experimented with all the forms of socialism that are proposed to us today. Greece, notably, put them all into practice and ended by dying of her dangerous experiments. The collectivist doctrines were exposed long ago in the *Republic* of Plato. Aristotle contests them, and as M. Guirand remarks . . . in his book *Landed Property Among the [Ancient] Greeks,* "All the contemporary doctrines are represented herein, from Christian socialism to the most advanced collectivism."

All the political revolutions in Greece were at the same time social revolutions, or revolutions with the aim of changing the inequalities of conditions by despoiling the rich and oppressing the aristocracy. They often succeeded, but their triumph was always ephemeral. The final result was the Hellenic decadence, and the loss of national independence. The socialists of those days agreed no better than the socialists of these, or, at least, agreed only to destroy—until Rome put an end to their perpetual dissensions by reducing Greece to servitude.

The Romans themselves did not escape from the attempts of the socialists. They suffered the experimental agrarian socialism of the Gracchi, which limited the territorial property of each citizen, distributed the surplus among the poor, and obliged the state to nourish the needy citizens. Thence resulted the struggles which gave rise to Marius, Sulla, the civil wars, and finally to the ruin of the Republic and the domination of the Emperors.

The Jews also were familiar with the demands of the socialists. The imprecations of their prophets, the true anarchists of their times, were above all imprecations against riches. Jesus, the most illustrious of them, asserted the right of the poor before everything. . . . "It is easier for a camel to go through the eye of a needle than for a rich man to enter the kingdom of God."

During the first two or three centuries of our era the Christian religion was the socialism of the poor, the disinherited, and the discontented; and, like modern socialism, it was in perpetual conflict with the established institutions. Nevertheless, Christian socialism ended by triumphing; it was the first time that the socialistic ideas obtained a lasting success.

But although it possessed one immense advantage— that of promising happiness only for a future life, and therefore of certainty that it could never see its promises disproved—Christian socialism could maintain itself only by renouncing its principles after victory. It was obliged to lean on the rich and powerful, and so to become the defender of the fortune and property it had formerly cursed. Like all triumphant revolutions, it became conservative in its turn, and the social ideal of Catholic Rome was not very far removed from that of Imperial Rome.

These seem very ancient, all these historical events which take us back to the Greeks, the Romans and the Jews; but in reality they are always young, for always they betray the laws of human nature—that human nature which, as yet, the course of ages has not changed. Humanity has aged much since then, but she always pursues the same dreams and suffers the same experiences without learning anything from them. Let anyone read the declaration full of hope and enthusiasm, issued by our [French] socialists of fifty years ago, at the moment of the revolution of 1848, of which they were the most valiant partisans. The new age was born, and, thanks to them, the face of the world was about to be changed. Thanks to them, their country sank into a despotism; and, a few years later, into a formidable war and invasion. Scarcely half a century has passed since this phase of socialism and, already forgetful of this latest lesson, we are preparing ourselves to repeat the same round.

The Theories of Socialism

The modern theories of social organization, under all their apparent diversity, lead back to two different and opposing fundamental principles—individualism and collectivism. By individualism, man is left to himself; his initiative is carried to a maximum and that of the state to a minimum. By collectivism a man's least actions are directed by the state, that is to say, by the aggregate; the individual possesses no initiative; all the acts of his life are mapped out. The two principles have always been more or less in conflict, and the development of modern civilization has rendered this conflict sharper than ever. . . . It is by gifted individuals, the rare and supreme fruits of a few superior races, that the most important discoveries and advances, by which all humanity profits, have been realized. The peoples among whom individualism is most highly developed are by this fact alone at the head of civilization, and today dominate the world. . . .

Modern socialism presents itself in a number of forms greatly differing in detail. By their general characteristics they rank themselves under the heading of collectivism. All would have recourse to the state to repair the injustice of destiny, and to proceed to the redistribution of wealth. Their fundamental propositions have at least the merit of extreme simplicity: confiscation by the state of capital, mines, and property, and the administration and redistribution of the public wealth by an immense army of bureaucrats. The state, or the community if you will—for the collectivists now no longer use the word state—would manufacture everything and permit no competition.

The least signs of initiative, individual liberty, or competition would be suppressed. The country would be nothing else than an immense monastery subjected to a strict discipline. The inheritance of property being abolished, no accumulation of fortune would be possible. . . .

Blinded as they are by their dreams, and convinced though they be of the superiority of institutions over economic laws, the more intelligent of the socialists have been obliged to understand that the great objections to their system are those terrible natural inequalities against which no amount of recrimination ever has been able to prevail. Except that there were in each generation a systematic massacre of all individuals surpassing by however little the lowest imaginable average, social inequality, the child of mental inequality, would quickly reestablish itself.

The theorists meet this objection by assuring us that in the new social environment thus artificially created, . . . the stimulant of personal interest, which has hitherto been the great motive of human nature and the source of all progress, would become useless and would be replaced by the sudden formation of altruistic instincts which would enable the individual to devote himself to the collective interest. It cannot be denied that religions, at least during the short periods of ardent belief following their birth, have obtained some analogous result; but they had heaven to offer to their believers, with an eternal life of rewards, while the socialists propose to their disciples in exchange for the sacrifice of their liberty only a hell of servitude and hopeless baseness.

To suppress the effects of natural inequality is theoretically an easy thing to do, but to suppress these inequalities themselves will always be impossible. They, with death and age, form a part of those eternal fatalities to which a man must submit himself.

The methods of realization proposed by the various socialist sects differ in form though all tend toward a common aim. They aim finally at obtaining an immediate state monopoly of the soil and of wealth in general. . . .

Today the program of the Christian socialists differs very little from that of the collectivists. But the other socialists repudiate them in their hatred of all religious ideas, and if revolutionary socialism were to triumph, the Christian socialists would assuredly be its first victims. . . .

Among the various sects [of socialism] that are born and die every day, anarchism deserves to be mentioned. Theoretically, the anarchists appear to come under the heading of individualists, since they desire to allow the individual an unlimited liberty; but in practice we must consider them merely as the extreme left of the socialist party, for they are equally intent on the destruction of the present social system. Their theories are characterized by that extreme simplicity which is the keynote of all socialist utopias: "Society is worthless; let us destroy it by steel and fire!" Thanks to the natural instincts of man they will form a new society—perfect, of course. By what train of astonishing miracles would the new society differ from those that have preceded it? That is what no anarchist ever has told us. It is evident, on the contrary, that if the present civilizations were to be completely destroyed, humanity would once again pass through all the forms it has perforce successively outgrown: savagery, barbarism, etc. . . .

Be it as it may, the anarchists and the collectivists are the only sects possessing any influence today. The collectivists imagine their theories were created by the German Karl Marx. As a matter of fact, we find them in detail in the writers of antiquity. Without going back so far, we may remark with Tocqueville [Alexis de, 1805–59], who wrote more than fifty years ago, that all the socialist theories are set forth at length in the *Code de la Nature* published by Morelly in 1755. . . .

Of all the errors that history has given birth to, the most disastrous, that which has uselessly shed the most blood and heaped up the greatest ruin, is this idea that a people, any people, can change its institutions as it pleases. All that it can do is to change the names of its institutions . . . to clothe with new words old concepts representing the natural outcome of a long past.

The Disciples of Socialism and Their Mental State

Socialism comprises many strongly differing and strongly contradictory theories. The army of its disciples have scarcely anything in common except an intense antipathy for the present state of things and vague aspirations toward a new ideal. . . . Although all the soldiers of this army appear to be marching together toward the destruction of the inheritance of the past, they are animated by strongly differing sentiments. . . .

At first sight, socialism would appear to draw the greater number of its recruits from the popular classes, and more especially from the working classes. The new ideal presents itself to them in the very elementary and therefore very comprehensible shape: less work and more pleasure. . . .

It would seem as though the popular classes could not hesitate in the face of promises so enticing and so often reiterated, above all when they hold all the reins in their hands, thanks to universal suffrage and the right to choose their legislators. Yet they do hesitate. The most astonishing thing today is not the rapidity but the slowness with which the new doctrines propagate themselves. . . .

One must know very little indeed of the workman to suppose him capable of pursuing seriously the realization of any ideal whatever, socialistic or otherwise. The ideal of the workman, when by chance he has one, is everything that is not revolutionary, not socialistic and everything that is middle class. . . .

The theorists of socialism think they know the mind of the working classes well; they really know very little about the matter. . . . The working classes, and still more the peasants, have the instinct of property at least as highly developed as the middle classes. . . .

Although he is headstrong, turbulent and always ready to side with the promoters of revolution, the working man is strongly attached to the old order of things; he is extremely arbitrary, a thorough conservative, and a firm believer in authority. He has always acclaimed those who shattered altars and thrones, but he has acclaimed with far greater fervor those who have reestablished them. When by chance he becomes employer in his turn, he behaves like an absolute monarch and is far harder on his former comrades than the middle class employer. . . .

As soon as he has a family, a house, and a few savings, the workman immediately becomes a stubborn conservative. The socialist, above all the anarchist-socialist, is usually a bachelor without home, means or family, that is to say, a nomad, and in all ages the nomad has been a refractory and a barbarian.

We may sum up . . . by observing that the class most refractory to socialism will be precisely the working class on which the socialists count so much. The socialists' propaganda has given rise to covetousness and hatred, but the new doctrines have not seriously affected the mind of the people. It is quite possible that the socialists may recruit from them the troops of a revolution, after one of those events which the working class always attribute to the government, such as a long period of unemployment or a fall in wages resulting from some economic competition; but it will be precisely these troops who will rally with all haste round the plume of the Caesar who will arise to suppress the revolution.

"A fact that largely aids the progress of socialism," writes M. de Laveleye, "is its gradual invasion of the upper and educated classes." The factors of this invasion, to my mind, are of several orders: the contagion of fashionable beliefs, fear, and indifference.

Socialistic tendencies today are far more prevalent among the middle classes than among the populace. They spread by simple contagion and with remarkable rapidity. Philosophers, men of letters and artists follow the movement with docility and contribute actively to spreading it. The theater, books, pictures even, are becoming more and more steeped in this tearful and sentimental socialism, which is entirely reminiscent of the humanitarianism of the controlling classes at the time of the revolution. The guillotine promptly taught them that in the struggle for life one cannot renounce self-defense without at the same time renouncing life. Considering the complacence with which the upper classes today are allowing themselves to be progressively disarmed, the historian of the future will feel only contempt for their lamentable want of foresight and will not lament their fate.

Fear is another of the factors which favor the propagation of socialism among the bourgeoisie. . . . They grope around irresolutely and hope to save themselves by concessions, forgetting that this is the most senseless policy imaginable, and that indecision, parleyings, and the desire to satisfy everybody are faults of character which, by an eternal injustice, the world has always punished cruelly, more cruelly than if they had been crimes.

Skeptical indifference, *"je m'en fichisme,"* . . . is the great malady of the modern bourgeoisie. When, to the declamations and assaults of an increasing minority, which is pursuing with fervor the realization of an ideal, nothing is set up in opposition, one may be sure that the triumph of the minority is very near at hand. Are the worst enemies of society those who attack it or those who do not even give themselves the trouble of defending it?

I apply the term *demi-savants* [half-scholars] to those who have no other knowledge than that contained in books, and who consequently know absolutely nothing about the realities of life. . . .

It is from the throng of *demi-savants,* notably of college graduates discontented with their lot, of leftovers from competitive examinations whom the state cannot employ, of university professors who find their merits overlooked, that the most dangerous disciples of socialism are recruited, and even the worst anarchists. . . .

. . . Their dream is to create by violent means a society in which they will be the masters. Their cry of equality does not prevent them from having an intense scorn of the rabble who have not, as they have, learned out of books. They believe themselves to be greatly the superiors of the working man, and are really his inferiors in their lack of practical sense and their exaggerated egotism. If they became masters, their despotism would be no less than that of Marat, Saint-Just, or Robespierre. . . .

To this category of *demi-savants* belong most often the *doctrinaires* who formulate in poisonous publications the theories which their ingenuous disciples promptly begin to propagate. . . . There is not a socialist who does not constantly invoke Karl Marx's *Das Kapital,* but I very much doubt that one in ten thousand ever has turned over the pages of this indigestible book. . . .

The *doctrinaire,* then, may be highly educated; that in no way saves him from being always obtuse and ingenuous, and most often an envious malcontent as well. Struck by only one side of a question, he remains in ignorance of the march of events and their recurrence. He is incapable of understanding anything of the complexity of social phenomena, of economic necessities, of atavistic influences, of the passions which really rule men. Having no guide but a bookish, rudimentary logic, he readily believes that his ideas are about to transform the evolution of humanity and overcome destiny. . . .

If one were to review the parts played by the various

classes in the dissolution of society among the Latin peoples, one would say that the *doctrinaires* and malcontents manufactured by the universities act above all by attacking ideals, and are, by reason of the intellectual anarchy they give rise to, one of the corrosive factors of destruction; the middle classes help the downfall by their indifference, their egotism, their feeble will and their absence of initiative or political preception; the lower classes act in a revolutionary way by seeking to destroy, so soon as it is sufficiently undermined, the edifice which is tottering on its foundations.

Tradition as a Factor of Civilization

Thanks to those few original minds to which every period gives birth, every civilization escapes little by little from the fetters of tradition; very slowly, it is true, because such minds are rare. This double necessity of fixity and variability is the fundamental condition of the birth and development of societies. A civilization becomes established when it creates a tradition, and it progresses only when it succeeds in modifying this tradition a little each generation. If it does not modify traditions, it does not progress. . . . The strength of the Anglo-Saxons consists in this: that while accepting the influence of the past they understand how to escape its tyranny in the necessary degree. The weakness of the Latins, on the contrary, is that they desire to reject the influence of the past, and incessantly to rebuild entirely all their institutions, beliefs and laws. . . .

The great danger of the present is that we have scarcely any common beliefs. Collective and identical interests are becoming further and further supplanted by dissimilar and particular interests. Our institutions, our laws, our arts, our education, have been established on beliefs which are crumbling every day, and which science and philosophy cannot replace; and of old it never was their role to do so. . . .

This extreme mobility of sentiments which are no longer directed by any fundamental belief renders them highly dangerous. In default of authority deceased, public opinion becomes more and more the master of all things, and, as it has at its service an all-powerful press to excite it or follow it, the role of the government becomes day by day more difficult, and the policy of statesmen more vacillating. . . .

The power of public opinion, so great and so fluctuating, extends not only to politics but also to all the elements of civilization. To artists it dictates their works, to judges their decrees, to governments their conduct. . . .

The power of the daily press has grown immeasurably; a power the more to be feared because it is without limit, without responsibility, without control, and is exercised by anonymous and absolute individuals. . . .

Will socialism be the new religion which shall come to substitute itself for the old beliefs? It lacks one factor of success: the magic power of creating a future life, hitherto the principal strength of the great religions which have conquered the world and which have en-

dured. All the promises of happiness offered by socialism must be realized here on earth. Now the realization
of such promises will clash fatally with the economic
and psychologic necessities over which man has no
power, and therefore the hour of the advent of socialism will undoubtedly be the hour of its decline.

The Conflict Between the Democratic Idea
and the Aspirations of the Socialists

Democracy, by its very principles, favors the liberty
and competition which of necessity lead to the triumph
of the most capable, while socialism, on the contrary,
aims at the suppression of competition, the disappearance of liberty, and a general equalization, so that there
is evidently an insuperable opposition between the
principles of socialism and those of democracy. . . .

Nothing could be less democratic than their [the
socialists'] desire to destroy the effects of liberty and of
natural inequality by an absolutely despotic regime
which would suppress all competition, give the same
salary to the capable and the incapable, and incessantly
destroy, by means of administrative measures, the
social inequalities which arise from natural inequalities. . . .

This conflict between the democratic idea and the
aspirations of the socialists is so far invisible to superficial minds, and most people consider socialism only
as the necessary development and foreseen conse-

quence of the democratic idea. In reality no two political conceptions are separated by deeper gulfs than socialism and democracy. . . . The divergency between the two doctrines is as yet hardly beginning to show itself, but it will soon be glaring, and then there will be a violent disruption.

It is not between democracy and science that there is and will be a real conflict, but between socialism and democracy. Democracy has indirectly given rise to socialism, and by socialism, perhaps, it will perish.

We must not dream, as some have done, of allowing socialism to attain its objective in order to prove its weakness, for socialism would immediately give birth to Caesarism, which would promptly suppress all the institutions of democracy. . . .

The taste for democracy is today universal throughout all nations, whatever be the form of their governments. We are, then, in the presence of one of those great social movements which it would be futile to seek to stem. The principal enemy of democracy at the present time, and the only one which could possibly overthrow it, is socialism.

The Sources and Division of Wealth: Intelligence, Capital and Labor

Practically the socialists recognize but two sources of wealth—capital and labor, and all their demands are directed against the part, according to them too

great, played by capital. Being unable to deny the
necessity of capital in modern industry, they dream of
the suppression of capitalists. But besides capital and
labor there is a third source of wealth—intelligence,
which the socialists consider to be of but little value.
Nonetheless, its action is predominant. . . . A socialist
recently assured the Chamber of Deputies that "there
are no such men as are in human reality the human
equivalent of a hundred thousand men." It is easy to
reply to him that in less than a century we can cite,
from Stephenson to Pasteur, a whole aristocracy of
inventors, each one of whom is worth far more than a
hundred thousand men, not only by the theoretical
value of his discoveries, but also by reason of the
wealth which his inventions have poured into the world
and the benefits which every worker has derived from
them. . . .

The socialists of every school are loath to admit the
importance of intellectual superiority. Their high priest
Marx understands by the term work nothing but manual labor, and relegates the spirit of invention, capacity
and direction, which has nevertheless transformed the
world, to a second place.

This hatred of intelligence on the part of the socialists is well founded, for it is precisely this intelligence
that will prove to be the eternal obstacle on which all
their ideas of equality will shatter themselves. Let us
suppose that by a measure analogous to the Edict of
Nantes—a measure which the socialists, were they the

masters, would very soon be driven to enforce—all the intellectual superiority of Europe—all the scientists, artists, great manufacturers, inventors, skilled workmen, and so forth, were expelled from civilized countries and obliged to take refuge in a narrow territory at present almost uninhabited—Iceland, for example. Let us further suppose that they departed without a halfpenny of capital. It is nevertheless impossible to doubt that this country, barren as it is supposed to be, would soon quickly become the leading country in the world for civilization and wealth. This wealth would soon be such that the exiles would be able to maintain a powerful army of mercenaries, and would have nothing to fear from any side. I do not think that such a hypothesis is altogether impossible of realization in the future.

Capital comprises all objects—merchandize, tools, plant, houses, lands, and so forth—having any negotiable value whatever. Money is only the representative symbol, the commercial unit, which serves to evaluate and exchange objects of various kinds.

For the socialists, work is the only source and measure of value. Capital would be merely a portion of unpaid work stolen from the worker.

It would be very foolish to waste time today in discussing assertions which have been so often refuted. Capital is work accumulated, either material or intellectual. It is capital that has freed man from the slavery of the Middle Ages, and above all from the slavery of nature, and which constitutes today the fundamental basis of all civilization. To persecute capital would be to oblige it to vanish or to conceal itself, and at the same stroke to kill industry, which it would no longer be able to support, and also to suppress wages. These are banalities that really require no demonstration.

The Conflict of Peoples and Classes

History teaches us . . . that the nations have always been struggling, have always continued to struggle, and that since the beginning of the world the right of the strongest has always been the arbiter of their destinies. That was the law of the past, and it is the law of the present. Nothing denotes that it will not be the law of the future also.

Not that there is today any lack of theologians and philanthropists to protest against it. To them we owe the numberless volumes in which they appeal, in eloquent phrases, to right and to justice as sovereign divinities directing the world from the depths of the skies. But the facts have always given the lie to their vain phraseology. These facts tell us that right exists only when it possesses the necessary strength to make itself respected. We cannot say that might is greater than right, for might and right are identical. No right can enforce itself without might. No one, I imagine, will doubt that a country which put its confidence in right and justice and disbanded its army would be immediately invaded, pillaged and enslaved by its neighbors. . . .

No nation must forget today that its rights are exactly limited by the forces at its disposal to defend those rights. . . .

We must recognize, as matter of daily observation, that human laws have been utterly powerless to modify the laws of nature, and that the latter continue to determine the relations of one people with another. All theories of right and justice are futile. International relations are today what they have been since the beginning of the world, when different interests are in question, or when it is merely a matter of a nation wishing to enlarge itself. Right and justice never have played any part in the relations of nations of unequal strength. . . . The phrases of diplomats and the sermons of orators remind one of the civilities uttered by men of the world when they have put their coats back on: The man of the world will stand aside to let you pass and will inquire with affectionate sympathy after your most distant relatives. But let any circumstance arise in which his interests are concerned and you behold these superficial sentiments vanish on the instant. . . .

We have very little reason to believe that the conflict of people with people will be less violent in the future than it has been in the past. On the other hand, there are very good reasons for believing that it will be far more violent. When nation was separated from nation by distances that science had not learned to bridge, the causes of conflict were rare. Today they are becoming more and more frequent. In the future, the principal motives of international conflict will be those great economic interests on which the very lives of nations depend.

The Struggle of Classes

The collectivists attribute to their high priest Karl Marx the statement . . . that history is dominated by the struggles of the different classes over matters of economic interests, and also the assertion that this struggle must disappear upon the absorption of all classes into one single class—the working class.

The first point, the struggle of the classes, is a banality as old as the world. By the mere fact of the unequal partition of wealth and power, caused by natural inequalities, or merely by social necessities, men have always been divided into classes of which the interests were necessarily more or less exposed and consequently at war. But the idea that this struggle might cease is one of those chimerical conceptions that are completely contradicted by the realities, and its realization is very far from being a desirable thing. Without the conflict of individuals, races and classes—in a world without universal conflict—man never would have emerged from savagery, would never have attained to civilization. . . .

And not only is there a struggle between the classes but also between the individuals of the same class, and the struggle among the latter, as in nature, is the most violent. The socialists themselves, although now and then united for a common end, which is the destruction of our present society, are unable to assemble together without the most violent discord.

The struggle today is more violent than it has ever been before, and this for many reasons; amongst them is that we have followed after chimeras of justice and equality which are unknown to nature. These empty formulae have done and will do more ill to man than all the ills which destiny has condemned him to suffer. . . .

Long before socialism, the religions had also the dream of suppressing the struggle of people with people, class with class, individual with individual, but what was the result of this endeavor save to make fiercer the very struggles they wished to abolish? Were not the wars they provoked the cruelest of all, the most fruitful of political and social disasters?

Can we hope that with the progress of civilization, the struggle of the classes will diminish? On the contrary, everything tends to show that it will become far more intense that it has ever been in the past. There are two reasons for this: the first is the more and more profound division between the classes; the second is the power which the new methods of association give to the various classes to defend their demands.

The first reason can hardly be contested. The differences between the classes of men and managers, proprietors and proletariat, for example, are visibly greater than the old differences of caste, say the difference between the people and the nobility. The distance created by birth, it was then considered, could not be bridged over. It was the result of the divine will and was accepted without discussion. Violent abuses might sometimes give rise to revolts, but the people revolted solely against the abuses and not against the established order of things. Today it is quite otherwise. The people revolt not against the abuses, which never were less than at present, but against the whole social system. . . .

The struggles of the future will be aggravated by the fact that they will not be inspired, as were the old wars of conquest, by the desire to pillage an enemy who, once conquered, became an object of indifference. Today furious hatred rages between the combatants, a hatred which is gradually tending to assume a religious form, and thus to acquire the special characteristics of ferocity and insubordination which invariably animate a true believer.

We have already perceived that one of the main causes of the present war of the classes is the extreme falsity of the ideas which the opposing parties have formed of one another. . . . Very often it is the very falsity of an idea which constitutes its strength. The most glaring error becomes for the crowd a radiant truth, if it be sufficiently repeated. Nothing is easier to sow than error, and when it has taken root, it has the omnipotence of the dogmas of religion. It inspires faith and nothing can stand against faith. In the Middle

Ages half of the West hurled itself on the East for the sake of the most erroneous concepts; by such errors the successors of Muhammad established their gigantic empire; by such errors Europe was later deluged with blood and fire. The falsity of the parent ideas of these upheavals is today evident to a child. Today they are merely vague words, the life of which the centuries have so exhausted that we can no longer understand the power they once exercised. Nonetheless, this power was irresistible, for there was a time when the clearest reason, the most obvious proofs were powerless to prevail against it. It is time only, and never reason, that has power to slay phantoms.

The Future Socialistic Struggles

The hour is approaching when the social edifice will suffer the most redoubtable assaults that have ever been made on it. The new barbarians are threatening not only the possessors of wealth, but also our very civilization, which appears to them to be merely the guardian of luxury and a useless complication. Never have the maledictions of their leaders been so furious; never has any people whose gods and thresholds were threatened by a pitiless enemy given vent to such imprecations. The more pacific socialists confine themselves to demanding the expropriation of the upper classes; the more zealous wish for their utter annihilation. . . .

Doubtless the past has seen struggles as violent, but the conditions of the opposing forces were very different and the defense of society a much easier matter. Then the crowd had no political power. . . .

The United States would seem fated to furnish the Old World with the first examples of the struggle which will take place between intelligence, capacity, capital and the terrible army of the unfit, . . . the social sediment which has been so greatly increased by the modern development of industry. . . .

The evolution of things has eroded the foundation of the edifice of the past ages. The army, the last pillar of the edifice, the only one that might yet sustain it, has entered on a process of disintegration and its worst enemies are now to be found in the educated classes.

The Social Solidarity

For many people, the term "social solidarity" always brings to mind, to some extent, the idea of charity. Its true sense, however, is very different. The societies of the present day are approaching solidarity of interests and relinquishing charity. It is even very probable that the societies of the future will regard charity as a low and barbarous conception, altruistic in nothing but appearance, thoroughly egoistic in essence, and generally noxious.

The term solidarity signifies merely association, and by no means charity or altruism. . . .

The movement in favor of solidarity, that is to say, the association of similar interests, which is so generally evident, is perhaps the most definite of the new social tendencies and is probably one of those that will have the greatest effect on our evolution. Today the word solidarity is heard far more often than the old shibboleths of equality and fraternity, and is tending to supplant them, though it is by no means synonymous. As the final aim of the association of interests is to struggle against other interests, it is evident that solidarity is only a particular form of the universal conflict of classes and individuals. Understood as it is today, solidarity reduces our old dreams of fraternity to the very closely circumscribed limits of associations. . . .

It is at once evident that a solidarity among individuals does not exist simply because they are engaged in a common enterprise, the success of which depends on the association of their efforts; indeed, we very often find the contrary. The director of a factory, his men, and his shareholders have theoretically a common interest in working for the success of the concern on which their existence or fortune depends. In reality this far-fetched solidarity covers only very conflicting interests. . . .

True solidarity is possible only among persons who have the same immediate interests. Such are the interests that have called into being the modern institution of the trade unions. . . .

The old relations, whether paternal or autocratic,

between employers and employees, masters and servants, are today done with. We may regret them, but only as we regret the dead, knowing well that we shall never behold them again. In the future evolution of the world, the mind will be ruled by interests, not by sentiments. Pity, charity and altruism are survivors without prestige or influence of a past that is dying before our eyes. The future will no longer know them.

The Fundamental Problem of Socialism: The Unadapted

Among the most important characteristics of our age we must mention the presence, in the midst of society, of a number of individuals who, for one reason or another, have been unable to adapt themselves to the necessities of modern civilization and are unable to find a place in it. They form a superfluity which cannot be utilized. They are the unadapted.

All societies have always possessed a certain number of these individuals, but their number never was so great as it is today. Unadapted to industry, science, the trades and the arts, they form an ever-increasing army. Notwithstanding their diversity of origin, they are united by one common sentiment—hatred of the civilization in which they can find no place. Every revolution, no matter what end it pursues, is certain to find them hurrying to join it at the first signal. It is among them that socialism finds its most zealous troops.

Their immense numbers, and their presence in all strata of society, render them more dangerous to modern society than were the barbarians to the Roman Empire. Rome was able to defend herself for a long time against outside invaders; but the modern barbarians are within our walls. The barbarians of antiquity envied the power of Rome, but they respected it. . . . Clovis was prouder of his title of Roman Consul than of his title King of the Franks.

The nations which disputed the succession of the Roman Empire were one and all anxious to maintain it to their own profit. Our new barbarians, on the contrary, will have nothing less than the destruction of the civilization of which they believe themselves to be victims. They aspire to its destruction and not to a conquest they would not know what to do with. If they did not burn Paris completely at the time of the Commune, it was only because their means were at fault. . . .

With the economic necessities dominating the modern world and competition the present law of production, things have undergone a profound change. As M. Cheysson very justly observes, "It is the triumph of individualism, freed from servitude, but destitute of guidance."

In the present period of transition, those who are unadapted through incapacity can hardly manage to live, however miserably. . . .

To the class of outcasts . . . we must add the hosts of

degenerates of all kinds—alcoholic, tuberculous, etc.—
who are preserved by modern medical science. It is
precisely these individuals who form almost the only
class which abandons itself without restraint to the
most disturbing fecundity, confirming the law I have
expounded that in the present period societies perpetu-
ate themselves above all by their lowest elements. . . .

To the host of the unfit created by competition and
degeneration must be added, as regards the Latin
nations, the degenerates produced by artificial incapacity. These artificial failures are made at great expense by our colleges and universities. The host of
graduates, licensees, instructors and professors without
employment will one day, perhaps, constitute one of
the most serious dangers against which society will
have to defend itself.

The men of each period live by a certain number of
political, religious or social ideas which are regarded as
indisputable dogmas of which they must necessarily
suffer the effects. One of the most powerful of such
ideas today is that of the superiority to be derived from
the theoretical instruction given in our colleges. The
schoolmaster and the university, rather looked down
on of old, have suddenly become the great modern
fetishes. It is they who are to remedy the inequalities
of nature, to efface the distinctions of class, and win
the battle for us. . . .

Although relatively limited, charity—whether public
or private—has hitherto done little except to increase

considerably the crowd of the unadapted. As soon as a state aid office is opened anywhere, the number of poor increases in enormous proportions. . . .

M. de Wateville wrote a few years ago in a report on the state of pauperism in France: "During the sixty years of existence of public home aid, it never has seen an indigent person emerge from his poverty and succeed in supplying his own needs through the assistance of this form of charity. On the contrary, it often causes hereditary pauperism. Thus we see today entered in the rolls of this department the grandsons of the indigents who were given public aid in 1802, while their sons, in 1830, were also on the fatal rolls. . . ."

The problem [of the "right to a job"] has long been occupying distinguished minds, and none of them has been able to find even a remote solution. It is evident that if a solution had been discovered, the social problem would in great measure have been solved.

It is because it remains so far unsolved that socialism, which pretends to resolve the insoluble problem, and which shrinks from no promises, is today so formidable. It has in its following all the vanquished and disinherited of the world, and all those unadapted whose formation we have noted. For them it [socialism] represents the last spark of hope that never dies in the hearts of men. But as its promises are necessarily in vain, and since the laws of nature that rule our fate cannot be changed, its impotence will become glaring to every eye in the very hour of its triumph, and it will

then have as its enemies the very multitudes it had seduced and who now place all their hope in it.

The Future of Socialism

Modern socialism is far more a mental state than a
doctrine. What makes it so threatening is not the very
insignificant changes which it has so far produced in
the popular mind, but the already very great changes
which it has caused in the mind of the directing classes.
The modern bourgeoisie are no longer sure of their
rights. Or rather they are not sure of anything, and
they do not know how to defend anything. They listen
to everything and tremble before the most pitiable
windbags. They are incapable of the firm will and the
severe discipline, of the community of hereditary sentiments, which are the cement of society and without
which no human association has hitherto been able to
exist. . . .

Social upheavals always are begun from above,
never from below. Was it the people who started our
great revolution? Not they indeed! They had never
dreamed of such a thing. It was let loose by the nobility
and the ruling class.

This very vague humanitarianism, a humanitarianism of words not of sentiments—the disastrous heritage of our old Christian ideas— . . . has become the
most serious element of success of modern socialism.
Under the unconscious but disintegrating influence of
this humanitarianism, the directing classes have lost

all confidence in the justice of their cause. They surrender more and more to the leaders of the opposing party, who merely despise them in proportion to their concessions; and the latter [the socialist leaders] will be satisfied only when they have taken everything from their adversaries, their lives as well as their fortunes. . . .

Before the hour of its triumph, which will be quickly followed by that of its fall, socialism is destined to widen its influence, and no argument drawn from reason will be able to prevail against it. . . .

The immediate fate of the nation which shall first see the triumph of socialism may be traced in a few lines. The people will of course begin by despoiling and then shooting a few thousands of employers, capitalists and members of the wealthy class. . . . Intelligence and ability will be replaced by mediocrity. The equality of servitude will be established everywhere. The socialists' dream being accomplished, eternal felicity should reign on earth and paradise descend.

Alas, no! It will be a hell, a terrible hell. . . .

A man is not a socialist without hating some person or thing. . . . Servitude, misery, and Caesarism are the fatal precipices to which all the roads of the socialists lead. Nevertheless, the frightful system would appear to be inevitable.

How Socialism May Be Opposed

The necessary work of defense is not to be undertaken with arguments capable of influencing the scientist or philosopher. . . .

It is not, I repeat, by such arguments that one can influence crowds. . . . To act on the crowd one must know how to work on their sentiments, and especially on their unconscious sentiments; and one must never appeal to their reason, for they have none. One must accordingly be familiar with their sentiments in order to manipulate them, and to be so one must be incessantly mixing with them, as do the priests of the new religion that is growing under our eyes.

Are they difficult to direct, these crowds? One must know but little of their psychology and history to think so. . . . Let us remember that history shows us that popular movements are in reality only the movements of a few leaders; let us remember the simplism of crowds, their immovable conservative instincts, and, finally, the mechanism of the . . . elements of persuasion: affirmation, repetition, contagion and prestige. Let us remember . . . that in spite of all appearances, it is not interest, powerful though it be in the individuals, that leads the crowd. The crowd must have an ideal, a belief, and before it becomes impassioned by its ideal or belief, it must become impassioned by its apostles. They and they only, by virtue of their prestige, awaken in the popular mind those sentiments of admiration which furnish the most solid basis of faith.

One can direct a crowd at will when one has the will. The most uncomfortable regimes, the most intolerant of despots, are always acclaimed by reason of the sole fact that they have succeeded in establishing themselves. In less than a century, the crowds have extended their suffrage to Marat, to Robespierre, to the Bourbons, to Napoleon, to the Republic, and to every chance adventurer as readily as to the great men. They [the crowds] accepted liberty and servitude with equal resignation.

In order to defend ourselves, not against the crowd but against its leaders, we have only to wish to do so. Unhappily, the great moral malady of our times, and one that seems incurable among Latins, is want of will. This decay of will, coinciding with the lack of initiative and the development of indifference, is the great danger which threatens us. . . .

It is of less importance to indicate what we ought to do than to indicate what we ought not to do. The social body is a very delicate organism which should be touched as seldom as possible. There is nothing more lamentable for a state than to be forever subject to the fickle and unreflecting will of the crowd. If one ought to do a great deal for the crowd, at least one ought to do very little by means of it. It would be an immense progress if we could merely give up our perpetual prospects of reform, and also the idea that we must always be changing our constitutions, our institutions, and our laws. Above all we ought to limit, and not constantly extend, the intervention of the state, so as to force the citizens to acquire a little of the initiative and the habit of self-government which they are losing through the perpetual tutelage that they cry for.

But once again, what is the use of expressing such wishes? . . . How can we hope for it? And, on the other hand, how can we resign ourselves to silence, when we foresee the dangers that are approaching, and when, theoretically, it appears easy to avoid them? If we allow doubt, indifference, the spirit of negation and criticism, and futile barren discussion and rivalries to increase their hold on us—if we continue always to call for the intervention of the state in the least affairs—we shall soon be submerged by the barbarians. . . .

Thus perished many civilizations of the past, when their natural defenders gave up struggle and effort. The ruin of nations has never been effected by the lowering of their intelligence, but by the lowering of their character. Thus ended Athens and Rome; thus ended Byzantium, the heir of the civilizations of antiquity. . . .

Let us strive not to imitate these descendants of ancient races, and let us beware of their fate. . . . Do not let us disdain the slightest effort, and let each contribute in his sphere, however modest it may be. Let us, without ceasing, study the problems with which the sphinx confronts us, and which we must answer under pain of being devoured by her. And when we think in our secret hearts that such advice is as vain, perhaps, as the hopeful vows made to an invalid whose days are numbered by fate, let us act as if we did not think so.

Part IV

The Evolution
of Matter

(L'Évolution de la Matière)

First edition published in Paris by E. Flammarion, 1905. Published in English in the United States by Charles Scribner's Sons, New York, 1907.

[Note: As already explained, Gustave Le Bon was in the habit of writing a preface or introduction to each of his major works and also additional explanatory material for subsequent editions. The following excerpts are taken solely from Le Bon's own remarks preceding his full text.

[These are offered as being of possible interest to scientists and students who might wish to become acquainted with the full text in view of the opinion expressed in 1906 by Francis Legge, British translator of *The Evolution of Matter* into English, that Le Bon's work in physics and chemistry might provide "many shrewd and pregnant hints" to scientists. Francis Legge was a prominent scholar and member of the Royal Institution of Great Britain, a renowned private organization dedicated to the advancement of science.]

Introduction (first edition)

This book is devoted to the study of the evolution of matter, that is to say, of the fundamental component of things, of the substratum of worlds and the beings that live on their surface.

It represents the synthesis of research experiments published during almost ten years in numerous papers. These have resulted in showing the insufficiency of certain fundamental scientific principles on which rest our knowledge of physics and chemistry.

According to the doctrine which seemed to be established for always and of which the formulation had demanded a century of persevering labor, while all things of the universe are condemned to perish, two elements alone—matter and energy—escape the fatal law. Endlessly transforming themselves, they nevertheless remained indestructible and in consequence immortal.

The facts put in evidence herein through my studies

and those which were deduced from them, show that—contrary to belief—matter is not eternal and can vanish without return. They likewise prove that the atom is the reservoir of a heretofore unsuspected energy which by its immensity goes beyond the forces that we know and is probably the origin of most other forces, notably of electricity and solar heat. Lastly, they [my studies] reveal that between the world of the ponderable and that of the imponderable, until now considered as profoundly separated, there exists an intermediate world. . . .

It is not without prolonged labor and heavy expenses that the facts assembled in this work were established. If I have not yet rallied the support of all scholars and if I have angered many of them by showing the fragility of dogmas possessing the authority of revealed truths, I nevertheless have encountered valiant defenders among eminent physicists and my studies have stimulated many others. One cannot ask for more, especially when one's work touches on principles of which several were considered as indisputable. It was not an ephemeral reality that the great Lamarck expressed when he said, "Whatever the difficulties in discovering new truths, those in gaining their recognition are greater."

Besides, I would possess but a very small amount of philosophy were I to remain surprised at the attacks of many physicists, and above all at the silence of those scholars who have made use of my experiments.

Gods and dogmas do not perish in a day. It went against all accepted ideas to try to prove that in all bodies the atoms thought to be eternal were not so. To try to show that matter, heretofore considered as inert, is the reservoir of a colossal energy, the probable source of most of the forces of the universe, was bound to shock still more accepted ideas. Demonstrations touching the very roots of our knowledge and shaking the secular edifice of science are generally met with anger or silence until the day when, having been repeated in detail by many researchers whose interest has been aroused, they have become so widespread and banal that it is almost impossible to point to their initiator.

It doesn't matter, in reality, that he who sows does not reap. It is enough that the crop grows. Among all the occupations able to fill the so brief hours of life, perhaps none is more worthy than the search for unknown truths, the opening up of new fields in the vast unknown with which we are enveloped.

Preface
(twenty-first thousand edition) *

"All new doctrine," writes the philosopher William James, "goes through three stages. It is attacked and declared absurd; then it is admitted as true and obvious but insignificant. Finally, its true importance is recognized and its adversaries claim the honor of having discovered it."

---

* So titled by the publisher since previous printings had totaled 21,000 copies.

This final phase is manifested the moment that an army of specialists intervenes. Each one adds a new observation or precise method of measurement. The name of the originator of the discovery is carefully avoided, except to misuse it, and if he does not defend himself a little, the fundamental facts he indicated are submerged in a flood of details complementing them.

The doctrine set forth in this work has known these three stages. Their progress was so rapid that the theories, once very new, now have become almost commonplace. . . .

When I first formulated these propositions and many others developed in this work, a great many physicists were angered. This sentiment did not come exclusively from the newness of the theories presented. It came also, according to the very correct observation of the scholarly physicist de Heen [professor of physics, University of Liege, Belgium], that professionals rarely admit that an important discovery can be made outside their ranks. History shows, however, that some most important principles of physics—the conservation of energy and that of Carnot, for example—are not to their credit. Telegraphy and photography and most of the great modern inventions did not come from their laboratories.

Preface
(twelfth edition)

The success of this work demonstrates the interest attached to scientific discoveries as soon as they appear to shed a little light on philosophical problems. Modern man has lost his old beliefs and he demands now from science new doctrines to orient his thinking.

Systems of philosophy were formerly built in the imagination of writers and never in the laboratories of savants. Today the old metaphysical speculations born of our dreams have lost all prestige. Their form still is seductive, but their arguments no longer captivate souls.

No civilization being able to live without an ideal, doctrines that perish always are replaced. If a new synthesis of the phenomena of the universe succeeds in being built on the debris of those that satisfied our fathers, probably it will emerge from the laboratories. It is in the temples of pure science that will be unveiled the secrets of the gods that olden times did not tell us. This is why faith in the power of science has become our latest belief. It seems evident that today we can understand nothing, know nothing and foresee nothing outside it.

Without doubt this growing divinity has revealed up to now only the relations of things and has not revealed to us their primary reason in a single phenomenon; but she is barely emerging from the shadows preceding her birth and the edifice of certainty is not built in a day.

This book, in which I tried to retrace the history of matter, to show that far from being eternal it is condemned to grow old and die, is a simple recital of my research experiments. Nevertheless the facts established bear so visibly on new interpretations concerning the origin of the worlds, their evolution and their end, that a piece of work done in the laboratory has ended by being a work of philosophy. Science and philosophy, once upon a time so distinct, tend to fuse themselves entirely. Soon they will not be separate things but one and the same thing.

Part V

Opinions and Beliefs

(Les Opinions et les Croyances)

First edition published in Paris by E. Flammarion, 1911.

Part I

The Problems of Belief and of Knowledge

The problem of belief, often confused with that of knowledge, is nevertheless strongly distinct from it. To know and to believe are different things not having the same genesis.

From opinions and beliefs derive our concept of life, our conduct, and consequently most of the happenings of history. These are governed, like all phenomena, by certain rules, but they are not yet well defined.

The domain of belief always has been surrounded by mysteries. That is why there are so few books about the origins of belief, while those about knowledge are innumerable. The rare efforts made to elucidate the problem of belief suffice, furthermore, to show how little it has been understood. Accepting Descartes' long-standing opinion, authors repeated that belief is rational and voluntary. An aim of this book is to show that it is neither voluntary nor rational.

The difficulty of the problem of belief didn't escape

the great Pascal. In a chapter on the art of persuasion, he correctly remarked that men "are almost always led to believe not by proof but by pleasure." He added, "But the pleasurable way is incomparably more difficult, more subtle, more useful and wonderful; also, if I do not deal with it, it is because I am not capable; and I feel myself so unequal to the task that I believe it to be absolutely impossible."

Thanks to the discoveries of modern science, it seems possible to us to approach the problem before which Pascal withdrew. Its solution furnishes the key to many important questions. How, for example, do religious and political beliefs establish themselves? How does one encounter the most naive superstitions in certain minds of very high intelligence? Why is reason so incapable of modifying our sentimental convictions? Without a theory of belief, these questions and many others remain insoluble. Reason alone cannot explain them. . . .

Ever since my first study of history, this problem has haunted me. Belief seemed to me to be the principal factor of history, but can one explain a fact so extraordinary as that the founding of beliefs determines the creation or fall of powerful civilizations?

Some nomad tribes, lost in the depths of Arabia, adopt a religion that an inspired leader teaches them, and owing to it they found within less than fifty years an empire as vast as Alexander's, an empire illustrated by a splendid array of marvelous monuments.

A few centuries earlier, semibarbarian people are converted to a faith preached by some apostles from an obscure corner of Galilee, and under the regenerating fires of this belief the old world crumbles and gives way to a new and different civilization in which every element remains impregnated with the memory of a God to which it has given birth.

Almost twenty centuries later, the old faith is shaken, unknown stars appear in the skies of thought, and a people arise who pretend to be able to break all ties to the past. Their destructive but powerful faith, despite the anarchy into which this great revolution plunges them, has the strength necessary to dominate Europe by force of arms and to make a victorious march across all its capitals.

How can one explain the strange power of beliefs? Why does man suddenly submit himself to a faith he knew nothing about yesterday, and why does it elevate itself so prodigiously above him himself? . . .

It is impossible to attribute intellectual weakness to men who voluntarily submit themselves to such a yoke because, from antiquity to our times, the same phenomena are observed in the most cultivated minds.

A theory of belief can be valid only if it brings the explanation of these things. It must above all lead to understanding of how the most illustrious scholars renowned for their critical minds accept legends so childishly naive as to be laughable. We conceive easily that a Newton, a Pascal, a Descartes, living in an atmosphere saturated with certain convictions, admitted them without discussion, in the same manner as they admitted the ineluctable laws of nature. But how is it that today, in circles where science sheds so much light, the same beliefs are not entirely disaggregated? Why do we see that when, by chance, they are disaggregated, other myths are immediately born, just as marvelous, as is proved by the propagation of occult doctrines, spiritualism, etc., among eminent savants? . . .

Let us try first of all to specify that which constitutes a belief and how it is distinguished from knowledge.

A belief is an act of faith of unconscious origin forcing us to admit as an entity an idea, an opinion, an explanation, a doctrine. As we shall see, reason is foreign to its formation. By the time a belief tries to justify itself, it is already formed.

Everything which is accepted by a simple act of faith must be qualified as a belief. If its exactitude is later verified by observation and experience, it ceases to be a belief and becomes knowledge.

Belief and knowledge constitute two strongly distinct modes of mental activity of very different origin. The first is an unconscious intuition that certain causes engender independently of our will; the second represents a conscious acquisition edified exclusively by rational methods, such as experience and observation.

It was only at an advanced stage of its history that humanity, plunged into the world of belief, discovered the world of knowledge. In penetrating it, all the phenomena formerly attributed to the will of superior beings were recognized as being subject to the influence of inflexible laws.

Owing solely to the fact that man approached the cycle of knowledge, all his former conceptions of the universe were changed. But it is not yet possible for him to penetrate very far into this new sphere. Science recognizes each day that its discoveries remain impregnated with the unknown. The most precise realities are surrounded by mysteries. A mystery is the unknown soul of things.

Science still is full of shadows and, behind the horizons it has attained, others appear, lost in an infinity which seems ever to recede.

The great domain which no philosophy has been able so far to illuminate is the kingdom of dreams. They are replete with hopes which no reasoning will be able to destroy. Therein all religious and political beliefs and other kinds of beliefs find limitless power. The unconquerable phantoms that inhabit it are created by faith.

To know and to believe always will be different things. While acquisition of even the slightest scientific truth requires enormous labor, the possession of a certitude having faith alone as its support requires none at all. All men possess beliefs; very few are able to elevate themselves to knowledge.

The world of beliefs has its own logic and laws. The scholar always has tried in vain to penetrate it with methods. One will see in this book why he loses all critical sense in penetrating into the cycle of belief and finds therein only the most deceptive illusions.

The Respective Roles of Belief and Knowledge

Knowledge constitutes an essential element in civilization, being the great factor in its material progress. Belief orients thoughts and opinions and, as a result, conduct.

Heretofore supposed to be of divine origin, beliefs were accepted without argument. We know now that they spring from within ourselves and yet they nevertheless impose themselves upon us. Reason has in general as little hold on them as on hunger or thirst. Elaborated in subconscious areas that intelligence cannot reach, a belief is undergone and is not arguable.

This unconscious and therefore involuntary origin of beliefs renders them very powerful. Whether religious, political or social, they always have played a preponderant role in history. Become general, they constitute the attracting poles around which gravitate people's existence and they put their stamp on all the elements of a civilization. One clearly describes this last by giving it the name of the faith that inspired it. Buddhist civilization, Muslim civilization, Christian civilization are very correct appellations.

It is in becoming the center of attraction that belief becomes also the center of deformation. The diverse elements of social life—philosophy, the arts, literature —modify themselves in order to adapt to it.

The only real revolutions are those which renew the fundamental beliefs of a people. They always have been very rare. Generally, it is in name only that a conviction is transformed. Faith changes its central object but never dies. It cannot die because the need to believe constitutes a psychological element as irreducible as pleasure and pain. The human soul has a horror of doubt and uncertainty. Man sometimes goes through phases of skepticism, but cannot dwell there. He needs to be guided by a credo—religious, political or moral—which dominates him and avoids for him the effort of thinking. Destroyed dogmas always are replaced. Reason has no hold on these indestructible necessities.

Our modern age has as much faith as the centuries that preceded it. Dogmas as despotic as those of the past are preached in new temples in which can be counted as many faithful as in the old. The old religious credo that previously enslaved the crowd is replaced by socialist or anarchist credos just as imperious and unreasonable but nevertheless dominating people's souls. The church may be replaced by the cabaret, but the sermons preached by mystical leaders are heard and received with the same faith.

And if the mentality of the faithful has not evolved much since that distant epoch when Isis and Hathor attracted thousands of fervent pilgrims to temples on the banks of the Nile, it is owing to the fact that down through the ages, feelings—the real foundation of the soul—maintain their fixity. Intelligence progresses, feelings do not change.

Without doubt, faith in any dogma is generally nothing but an illusion. Nevertheless one must not disdain it. Thanks to its magical power, the unreal becomes more potent than the real. An accepted faith gives to a people a community of thought generating their unity and force.

The field of knowledge being very different from that of belief, it is useless to oppose one to the other, though attempted daily.

Science, disengaged more and more from belief, remains nevertheless heavily permeated by it. Science is subjected to belief in all poorly known fields—the mysteries of life or the origin of the species, for example. The theories that are accepted are simple articles of faith enjoying only the authority of the masters who formulate them.

The laws controlling the psychology of belief are applicable not only to the great fundamental convictions which left an indelible stamp on the course of history. They also are applicable to most of our daily opinions on the beings and things that surround us. Observation shows easily that the majority of these opinions are not supported by rational elements, but by affective or mystical ones generally of an unconscious nature. If one sees them debated with such ardor, it is precisely because they arise from the field of belief and are formed in the same way. In general, opinions represent little beliefs more or less transitory.

It would be an error to believe that one emerges

from the field of belief by renouncing ancestral convictions. . . .

The questions raised by the genesis of opinions being of the same order as those relating to belief, they should be studied in the same way. Often distinct in their effects, beliefs and opinions nevertheless belong to the same family, while knowledge is part of a completely different world. . . .

Part II

The Affective Self and the Intellectual Self

In studying the determining motives of our opinions and beliefs, we shall see that they are ruled by distinct forms confused up to now.

Before undertaking their examination, I shall insist on a fundamental separation of the psychic elements which dominate all others. Actually, these are presented in two very different forms: the affective elements and the intellectual elements. Ignorance of the difference is one of the most frequent causes of error in our judgments. Legions of politicians have wished to base on reasoning that which can be based only on feelings. Historians too, also unenlightened, have thought it possible to explain with intellectual logic facts completely foreign to its influence. . . . Most psychologists still persist in the same error. . . .

The affective self and the rational self act incessantly

upon each other while having an independent existence. Because the affective self evolves despite ourselves and often in spite of ourselves, life is full of contradictions. It is possible sometimes to restrain our feelings but not to make them be born or disappear.

It is for this reason that we reproach an individual for having changed. This reproach rests on the accepted but very false idea that intelligence can modify a feeling. That is a complete mistake. When love becomes indifference or antipathy, for example, intelligence assists in the change but is not the cause. The reasons imagined to explain such alterations have no relation to the true motives. These we do not know.

"Frequently," says [Theodule] Ribot, "one imagines a profound and solid attachment to a person (love, friendship); absence or the necessity of a rupture demonstrates its fragility. Inversely, absence or a rupture reveals to us a profound affection that seemed mild or almost indifferent." It is therefore impossible, remarked the same author, to judge the intellectual self by the conduct of the affective self.

Even though affective life and intellectual life are too heterogeneous to be melded into each other, one always acts without taking into full account the difference that separates feelings and intelligence. . . . The conviction that the development of intelligence through education also develops feelings, and that the association builds character, is one of the most dangerous prejudices of our universities. English educators have known for a long time that the education of character is not done by books.

The affective and intellectual self being entirely distinct, it is not surprising that a very high intelligence can exist along with a very bad character. Without doubt, intelligence and education show that certain dishonest acts cost more than they are worth, and one rarely sees a learned man commit ordinary burglaries. But if he possesses the soul of a thief, he will retain it despite all his diplomas and will use it in less dangerous immoral operations with surer profit. . . .

In all transitory collectivities the same distinction between the affective and intellectual is easier to observe. The elements putting them together and dictating their acts are feelings and never intelligence. I have explained the reasons for this in another work [*The Psychology of the Crowd*]. It suffices to say that intelligence, varying considerably from one individual to another, is unlike feelings and is not contagious. On the other hand, individuals of the same race possess certain common feelings easily fused when they form a group.

The affective self constitutes the most fundamental element of a personality. It has been very slowly elaborated during ancestral acquisitions and its evolution in individuals and peoples is much slower than that of intelligence.

This thesis seems at first to be contradicted by history. It would seem that at certain times feelings arise which are quite different from those previously observed. Bellicose at one time, a nation seems pacific at others. The need for equality follows previous acceptance of inequality. Skepticism replaces ardent faith. There are numerous examples of the same sort.

Analysis of them shows that these creations of new feelings are simple semblances. In reality, the feelings existed without manifesting themselves; it was only variations of surroundings or circumstances that modified their balance. A feeling curbed in one epoch becomes preponderant in another and dominates in a more or less durable way the other affective conditions. A man is obliged to adapt his feelings to the successive necessities imposed by circumstances and above all by the social climate. . . .

The feelings sometimes seem to have changed, whereas they merely are applied to different subjects. The modern workman's mystical hopes guiding him to a smoke-filled bar where the apostles of a new evangel promise him an imminent paradise are the same sentiments that led his fathers to the old cathedrals where, behind a haze of incense, golden doors opened to luminous regions filled with eternal joy.

The Divers Manifestations of Affective Life: Emotions, Feelings, Passions

The manifestations of affective life are indiscriminately designated by authors under the names of emotions or feelings. I believe it to be a more convenient description to assort them into three classes: emotions; feelings; passions.

An emotion is an instant feeling more or less ephemeral. It is born of a sudden phenomenon: an accident, news of a catastrophe, a threat, an insult, etc. Anger, fear and terror are emotions.

A feeling represents a lasting affective, such as goodness, helpfulness, etc.

A passion consists of feelings which have acquired great intensity able momentarily to nullify all others: hate; love; etc.

All these affective states correspond to physical variations of our organism. We know only a few general effects: blushing, changes in circulation [of blood], etc. A physical or chemical change of nerve cells and the feelings it engenders represents a relationship of which only the ultimate results are known. The transformation of a feeling or a thought by an organic chemical process is completely inexplicable at the present time.

Feelings and emotions vary according to the physiological state of the individual or the influence of different excitants: coffee, alcohol, etc. The most simple feeling often is very complicated, but as soon as it becomes differentiated from another by analysis, we should, for linguistic convenience, treat it as if it were simple. The chemist too treats as simple compounds those which he cannot break down.

Psychologists sometimes talk about intellectual feelings. . . . I cannot admit this theory which confuses
cause with effect. A feeling can be produced by influences as diverse as the action of a pleasurable food or
that of a scientific discovery, but it always remains a
feeling. The most we can say is that our ideas have an
emotional equivalent. Even numbers have one; as
[Henri] Bergson has correctly observed: "Merchants
understand this very well, and instead of indicating the
price of an object in a round number of francs, they
mark it with an immediately inferior number."

A feeling become preponderant and persistent takes,
as we have said, the name of passion. Up to now,
psychologists have not yet been able to define or
classify the passions. Spinoza admitted three: desire,
joy and grief, from which all others could be deduced.
Descartes admitted six primitive passions: admiration,
love, hate, desire, joy and grief. Obviously, these are
solely forms of language incapable of explaining anything and not sustainable by argument.

A passion can be born suddenly, like love at first
sight [*coup de foudre*], or by slow incubation. Once
constituted, it dominates both the affective and intellectual life. Reason generally has no action on it and
merely puts itself at its service. . . .

When intelligence succeeds in exercising an inhibiting influence over passion, the latter is not very strong.
Intelligence can only act against passion by opposing
one mental image of a feeling against another. The

struggle exists then, not between intellectual and affective images, but uniquely between affective images put
together by intelligence.

Affective Memory

Memory of feelings exists as does that of intelligence,
but to a much lesser degree. Time weakens it very
quickly.

The customary inferiority of affective memory to
intellectual memory is generally considerable. The
persistence of the latter is such that, for centuries,
voluminous works such as the Vedas and songs of
Homer were transmitted from generation to generation
only with the aid of memory. In times when books
were rare and costly, in the thirteenth century for
example, students knew how to retain the courses that
were recited to them. . . .

If memory of feelings were as tenacious as intellectual memory, the persistent remembrance of our suffer-
ings would render life unendurable.

To the theory of the short duration of affective
memory, one could oppose the persistence of class
hatreds and race hatreds over many generations. This
apparent duration is merely an incessant renewal produced by continually repeated causes. An unnourished
hatred does not endure. That of the Germans for the
French would have disappeared long ago if German
newspapers had not constantly stirred it up. . . .

The Russian Alliance and the Anglo-French Entente

show how quickly peoples who were former enemies forget hatreds not nourished. When Britain became our friend, however, we were not far from the terrible humiliation of Fashoda.

This concept of the essential brevity of affective memory explains many phenomena in the life of peoples. One must not count on their gratitude, but also one must not dread too much their hatred.

The Elements of Character

Character is composed of an aggregate of affective elements on which are superimposed, while being only very slightly mingled, some intellectual elements. It is always the former that give an individual his true personality.

The affective elements being numerous, their association forms various kinds of character: active, reflective, apathetic, sensitive, etc. Each of them behaves differently under the action of similar stimulants.

The aggregates forming character can be strongly or feebly cemented together. Solid aggregates correspond to strong individualities able to maintain themselves despite variations in surroundings and circumstances. Poorly cemented aggregates correspond to weak mentalities, uncertain and changeable. They would modify themselves from moment to moment under the slightest influences if certain necessities of daily life did not orient them, as the banks of a river confine its course. . . .

Moral causes act on character or at least on its orientation. Following a conversion profane love becomes divine love. A fanatical and persecuting clergyman sometimes ends up as a free thinker equally fanatical and not less persecuting.

Opinions and beliefs being molded on our character, they naturally follow its variations.

There does not exist . . . any parallelism between the development of character and that of intelligence. The former, on the contrary, tends to become weakened as the latter develops. Great civilizations were destroyed by inferior intellectual elements endowed with strong will.

Courageous, decisive minds ignore the obstacles signaled by intelligence. Reason does not found great religions and powerful empires. In societies brilliant with intelligence but of weak character, power ends by falling into the hands of narrow-minded bold men. I agree with Faguet that a pacifist Europe will be conquered "by the last people remaining military and relatively feudal." Such a people will reduce the others to slavery and will put to forced labor for their profit all the pacifists loaded with intelligence but void of energy born of will.

The Collective Characteristics of Peoples

Each people possesses collective characteristics common to most of its members, which is what makes veritable psychological species of different nations.

These characteristics create . . . similar opinions among them on a certain number of essential subjects.

The fundamental characteristics of a people are not necessarily numerous. Firmly fixed, they mark its destiny. Let us consider the English, for example. The elements directing their history can be summed up easily in a few lines: the cult of persistent effort preventing retreat in the face of obstacles and consideration of a calamity as irremediable; a religious respect for traditions and for all that has been validated by the passage of time; a need for action and disdain of idle speculative thought; an intense sense of duty; self-control regarded as an essential quality and carefully maintained by special education.

Certain defects of character insupportable in individuals become virtues when collective—pride, for example. This feeling is very different from vanity. . . . Collective pride is one of the great stimulants of a people's activity. Due to it, the Roman legionary found full compensation in being a part of a people dominating the universe. The unflinching courage of the Japanese during the last war [Russo-Japanese] came from similar pride. This sentiment, besides, is a source of progress. As soon as a nation is convinced of its superiority, it carries to the maximum the effort necessary to maintain it.

It is character and not intelligence that distinguishes peoples and creates irreducible antipathies or sympathies among them. Intelligence is the same for all.

Character, on the contrary, offers strong differences. Peoples being differently impressed by the same things will conduct themselves differently under apparently identical circumstances. Moreover, whether peoples or individuals are concerned, men always are divided more by the contrasts of their character than by those of their interests or intelligence.

The Evolution of Elements of Character

The fundamental feelings forming the web of character evolve slowly over the ages, as is proved by the persistence of national characteristics. The psychological agglomerations forming them are as stable as the anatomical agglomerations.

But around these fundamental characteristics are found in all living beings secondary characteristics which can vary according to the times, environment, etc. It is above all . . . the subjects on which feelings are exercised that change. Love of family, of tribe, of city and country are adaptations of an identical feeling for different groups and not the creation of new feelings. Internationalism and pacifism represent the latest extensions of the same feeling.

A little less than a century ago, German patriotism was unknown. Germany was divided into rival provinces. If today pan-Germanism is a virtue, that virtue is merely the extension of ancient feelings to new categories of individuals.

Affective states are so stable that their simple adaptation to new subjects requires immense effort. To acquire, for example, a little, a very little of that quality of altruism known as tolerance, it was necessary, says Lavisse correctly, "that martyrs died by the thousands under torture, and that blood flowed in rivers on battle-fields."

It is very dangerous for a people to wish to create by means of reason feelings which are contrary to those fixed by nature in their soul. This kind of error weighs heavily on us since the [French] Revolution. It engendered the development of socialism which pretends to be able to change the natural course of things and remake the soul of a nation. . . .

And if, at present, the future seems very dark, it is because the feelings of the masses are tending to undergo new orientation. Under the growth of socialist illusions, everyone—from the workman to the professor—has become dissatisfied with his lot and is persuaded that he merits a different fate. Each workman believes himself to be exploited by the ruling classes and dreams of seizing their wealth by force. In the realm of the affective, illusions have a strength that renders them very dangerous because reason does not affect them.

The Disaggregation of Character and the Oscillations of Personality

We have said that the stability of aggregates forming character is as great as that of anatomical aggregates.

The former, like the latter, can undergo morbid changes and even complete disaggregation. These phenomena, which do not arise exclusively in the realm of pathology, have considerable influence on the formation of opinions and beliefs. . . .

Under various disturbances, represented by motives, the combinations forming character can be modified. Then our sensibilities change; the orientation of life becomes different. The personality is renewed.

Such variations are observed above all when—the balance established between affective elements and surroundings having undergone sudden change—the social environment is strongly altered. . . .

Any being, whether inert or living matter, is the result of a certain balance between environment and itself. The latter cannot change without a simultaneous change in the former. A rigid steel bar can, under the influence of a suitable environment, become a light vapor.

The degree of the tendency of disassociation of psychic elements forming character depends on the stability of the latter as well as on the important environmental changes to which they are subjected. Also, they will vary following previously undergone impressions. Observations made about anatomical aggregates are also valid for psychological aggregates. The lessening of the sensibility of the former under the influence of certain exterior influences is called, as we know, immunization. Future study of the pathology of [psychological] characteristics also will comprise that of their immunization.

The true statesman possesses the art, still a mystery, of knowing how to modify some elements of national character for the sake of balance in order to make them predominate according to the necessities of the times.

The Oscillations of Personality

The foregoing considerations tend to show that our personality can become quite variable. It depends, in effect, on two inseparable factors: the being itself and its environment. . . .

Our self is a total. It is the sum of innumerable self cells. Each cell competes with the unity of the whole, in the same manner as a soldier does in an army. The homogeneity of thousands of individuals of which it is composed is the result only of their community of action that numerous causes can destroy.

It is useless to object that people's personality seems in general quite stable. If it seems hardly to vary, it is because the social environment remains just about constant. But if it is suddenly modified, as in the time of revolution, a person's personality can change entirely. It is thus that one saw, during the [Reign of] Terror, good kindly bourgeois become bloodthirsty fanatics. The torment gone and the former environment restored, they recovered their peaceful personality. . . .

What are the elements composing the self of which

the synthesis forms our personality? Psychology remains silent on the subject. Without pretending to be too precise, we shall say that all the elements of self are the result of a residue of ancestral personalities, that is to say, they were created by their previous existences. The self, I insist, is not a unity but a total of millions of cellular lives composing the organism. These can engender innumerable combinations.

Violent emotional excitements, certain observable pathological states among [spiritualist] mediums, ecstatics, hypnotized individuals, etc., can evoke some of these combinations and obtain, at least momentarily, a different personality in the same person, either inferior or superior to the usual personality. Each of us possesses possibilities of action going beyond our normal capacity that certain circumstances can awaken.

Ancestral residues form the most profound and stable layer of character in peoples and individuals. It is in their ancestral self that an Englishmen, a Frenchman, a Chinese differ so profoundly. But on these far away atavisms are overlaid elements engendered by social milieu (caste, class, profession, etc.), by education and by many other influences. These lend a quite stable orientation to our personality. It is on this somewhat artificial self that we lead our everyday lives.

Among all the elements forming our personality, the most active, after that of race, is that which is determined by the social group to which we belong. . . .

The tyranny of social groups . . . is not useless. If men didn't have the opinions and conduct of their own circle as a guide, where would they find the mental direction most of them need? Thanks to the group in which they are embedded, they possess a rather constant way of acting and reacting. Thanks also to it, people of rather spineless nature are oriented and sustained in life.

Thus canalized, the members of an ordinary social group possess along with a temporary or lasting but quite definite personality a power for action which no individual member dreamed of. The great massacres of the Revolution were not the work of individuals. Their authors acted in groups: Girondists, Dantonists, Hébertists, Robespierrists, Thermidorians, etc. It was these groups rather than individuals who fought one another. They had then to bring to their struggle the furious ferocity and narrow-minded fanaticism characteristic of demonstrations by violent collectivities.

Difficulty of Predicting Conduct

The self being variable and dependent on circumstances, no man ought to pretend to know another. He can only assert that when circumstances do not vary, the conduct of a given individual will hardly change. The head of a bureau, having directed it honestly for twenty years will doubtless continue to do so with the same honesty, but one must not count too much on this. New circumstances having erupted—a passion overcoming his good sense, a danger menacing his home—the insignificant bureaucrat can become a scoundrel or hero.

The great changes in personality occur mostly in the sphere of feelings. In that of intelligence, the changes are very slight. An imbecile will always be one.

The possible variations of personality which prevent our knowing others also prevent us from knowing ourselves. The ancient philosophers' adage "Know thyself" is unrealizable. . . . The exterior self usually represents a personage of assumed untruth. This is so, not only because we imagine ourselves to be endowed with many good qualities and do not recognize our faults, but also because though the self contains a small portion of conscious elements, it is for the most part formed of unconscious elements inaccessible to observation.

The only means of discovering one's real self . . . is in one's actions. One knows oneself a little after having observed one's own conduct in given circumstances. To pretend to know in advance how we will behave in a given situation is deceptive. When Marshal Ney swore to Louis XVIII to bring him Napoleon in an iron cage, he was of good faith but didn't know himself. One look from the master was enough to melt his resolve. The unhappy marshal paid with his own life

for his ignorance of his own real personality. Had Louis
XVIII been more familiar with the laws of psychology,
he probably would have pardoned him. . . .

The theories set forth in this book pertaining to
character sometimes seem contradictory. On the one
hand, we have insisted on the fixity of sentiments forming character, and on the other we have shown the
possible variations of personality. These contradictions
disappear when bearing in mind the following points:

1. Characteristics are formed by an aggregate of
   almost unchanging fundamental affective elements to which are added easily changed accessory elements. These last correspond to the modifications that the art of the stock-breeder makes
   a species undergo without altering the essential
   characteristics [of the species].

2. Like anatomical species, psychological species
   depend narrowly on their milieu. They must
   adapt themselves to all changes in that milieu and
   indeed they do adapt themselves providing the
   changes are neither too considerable nor sudden.

3. The same sentiments appear to change when directed toward different subjects, yet their real
   nature has not undergone any modification whatsoever. Profane love which has become divine
   love in certain conversions is a sentiment which
   has changed its name but not its nature.

All these findings are of very practical interest since

they are the very basis of several important modern problems, notably that of education.

Believing that this last modifies intelligence, or at least the sum of our individual knowledge, it was concluded that it could also modify feelings. This was to forget entirely that affective and intellectual states have no parallel evolution.

The deeper one goes into the subject, the more one is obliged to acknowledge that education and political institutions play a rather weak role in the destiny of individuals and peoples.

This doctrine, contrary, by the way, to our democratic beliefs, seems sometimes to contradict the facts observed among certain modern peoples and that is what will always prevent its easy acceptance. In the introduction which he wrote to the Japanese translation of my works, one of the most eminent statesmen of the Far East, Baron Motono, [Japanese] Ambassador to St. Petersburg [Russia], pointed out in objection the many changes produced in the Japanese mentality by the influence of European ideas. Nevertheless, I do not believe that these prove a genuine modification of this mentality. The European ideas simply entered into the ancestral armature of the Japanese soul without modifying its essential aspects. The substitution of insurrection for religious rule [as in the French Revolution] could completely alter the destiny of a people without transforming its national character.

Part III

The Classification of Various
Forms of Logic

Logic has been considered until now to be the art of reasoning and proof. But to live is to act, and proof is not the most frequent motivator of action.

The diverse forms of vital and psychological action . . . are governed by very different forms of logic.

Action constituting in our opinion the sole criterion of logic, we shall see how different logics lead to dissimilar results.

In studying an ordinary act, the psychologist ought not to look only at the end pursued or means employed, nor at the success or failure. The only interesting elements are the generating motivations of the act. There are virtuous or criminal actions, useful or useless ones, but there are no illogical ones. They are simply sprung from different logics and none can serve exclusively in judging the others. . . .

One can, I believe, establish five forms of logic: (1) biological logic; (2) affective logic; (3) collective logic; (4) mystical logic; and (5) rational logic. . . .

We shall briefly examine their nature:

Biological logic: . . . Let us simply say that biological logic, which presides over beings and the creation of their forms, bears no trace of influence by our will, but produces adaptations in a determined direction by forces unknown to us. These forces seem to act as if they possessed reason superior to ours and are not at all mechanical since their action varies every moment according to the need served.

The addition of biological logic to the other forms, which dominates them from far above, only fills in a blank concealed by the old metaphysical theories.

Affective logic: Until now, psychologists recognized only rational logic. They have begun to add affective logic, or that of feelings, which is absolutely distinct from rational logic. These two forms of logic differ above all in that intellectual associations can be conscious, whereas those of affective states remain unconscious. Affective logic directs most of our actions.

Collective logic: This form of logic is the result of a particular state of mind called mystic. In the early stages of man it was universal and still is widespread. To the mystical mind, the sequence or chain of things has no regularity; it depends on superior beings or forces to which we must submit our will.

Mystical logic has always determined a great number of most men's actions. It is different from the unconscious logic of feelings, not only because it is conscious and comprises deliberations, but also and above all because it can engender under its influence actions diametrically opposed to those dictated by affective logic.

Rational logic: This logic is the art of voluntarily associating mental images and perceiving their analogies and differences, that is to say, their relationships.

It is just about the only one to which psychologists have paid attention. Since Aristotle, innumerable books have been consecrated to it.

Coexistence of the Different Forms of Logic

All forms of logic can superimpose themselves on one another, fuse themselves or combat one another in the same beings. Depending on the times and races, one of them succeeds in predominating but never can entirely eliminate the others.

Affective logic led an Athenian general, jealous of his rivals, to declare war on them. Mystical logic made him consult oracles concerning the best time to undertake military operations. Rational logic guided his tactics. During all his acts, biological logic made him live. . . .

If the study of a science as exact as physics requires hypotheses, one should not be astonished at seeing that we must proceed in the same manner in a much more complicated science, namely, psychology.

The physicist does not claim that the ether exists. He simply says that things take place as if the ether existed and that all phenomena would be incomprehensible without this supposed existence.

We do not affirm that there exist forms of logic constituting distinct entities; we simply say that things happen as if they really existed.

Part IV

The Conflict of Different Forms of Logic

The superimposition of different forms of logic within the same individual explains immediately a problem which always has been embarrassing. How is it that superior minds, accustomed to rigorously applied scientific methods, can accept religious, political, spiritual or occultist beliefs which, in the face of rational logic disengaged from all extraneous elements, cannot withstand scrutiny?

The answer is, in reality, quite simple. In their scientific concepts, these minds are guided by rational logic. In their beliefs, they obey the laws of mystical or affective logic.

A scholar passes from the sphere of knowledge to that of belief as if he were changing residence. The error of which he often is victim consists in his wanting to apply to mystical or affective logic the methods of intellectual logic with the aim of giving scientific basis to his beliefs.

The equilibrium among different forms of logic being upset, they enter into conflict. In this conflict, rational logic rarely wins. It easily permits itself to be tortured, by the way, in order to place itself at the service of the most childish concepts. That is why, in matters of religious, political or moral belief, all dispute is useless. To debate rationally a mystical or affective belief with someone serves only to exalt it. To debate it within oneself doesn't shake it further except when it has arrived at such a degree of erosion that it no longer has any strength. . . .

. . . Thanks to its ability to associate affective and intellectual images, intelligence can sometimes make use of feelings in the same manner as an architect can use the same kinds of stone to build different edifices.

The action of intelligence on feelings is not limitless, indeed it seems quite restricted. Observation shows, in effect, that if the latter are very intense, the former loses all power. The force of certain sentiments can become such that not only intelligence but also the most evident self-interests of the individual remain without influence. . . .

If feelings are not directly transformed into ideas, they nevertheless are the creators of ideas, and, in turn, become evocative of other feelings. Thus while preserving their independence, these two spheres of mental activity constantly act upon each other. Ideas therefore exert an undeniable action on our individual and collective life, even if indirectly; but, I repeat, their role is possible only on condition that they rest on an affective substratum. Ideas arise from feelings, and the conflicts between ideas are, in reality, only conflicts between feelings. People who seem to be fighting for ideas are really fighting for feelings from which the ideas are derived.

Affective states not having the opportunity to become externalized lose not their existence but their strength, like all unused organs. . . .

Often ignored by educators, this law that a feeling not exercised withers away seems to have general application. The history of peoples furnishes many examples. Our warrior instincts, so highly developed at the time of the Revolution and the Empire, are giving way each day to a more widespread pacifism and antimilitarism not only among the masses but also among the intellectuals. There results the following very strange contrast: As nations become more pacific, their governments constantly increase armaments.

The reason for this apparent anomaly is simple: The individuals obey their personal egoism; while governments are obliged to be preoccupied with the collective interest. More enlightened than the crowd and their leaders, they [governments] know from secular experience that every nation which weakens itself is soon invaded and pillaged by its neighbors. Modern nations can no more escape from this law than their predecessors in antique civilizations. The Poles, Turks, Egyptions and Serbs, etc., were able to avoid destructive invasions only by permitting themselves to be despoiled of all or part of their territory. . . .

All primitives—savages, animals, etc.—tend constantly to give free rein to their instincts. Nevertheless, as soon as the former live in tribes and the latter are domesticated, necessity forces them to restrain a few. They succeed only by opposing a very strong feeling—

fear of punishment, hope of recompense, for example
—to another feeling to which impulse tempts them to
succumb.

The ability to dominate affective impulses represents
the fundamental attribute of a civilization. No social
life is possible without this essential basis of all morality. . . .

All civilization implies discomfort and constraint.
In learning to control his impulses a little according to
the rigorous laws of first social obligations, the primitive disengages himself from pure animality and attains
barbarism. Forced further to restrain himself, he elevates himself to civilization. This last maintains itself
only for so long as man controls himself. . . .

Feelings reined in by social necessities codified into
laws are not destroyed. Delivered from their bonds,
primitive natural impulses always reappear. This explains the violence that accompanies revolutions. The
civilized man returns to barbarism. . . .

One does not liberate feelings that the social milieu
had with great difficulty succeeded in restraining without creating anarchy. Its first symptom is a rapid increase in criminality . . . It is in turn favored by the
development of humanitarianism which paralyzes repression and tends, as a result, to destroy all brakes.

Our democracy is actually experiencing more and
more the consequences of the suppression of its inhibiting actions which alone could counter-balance
antisocial feelings. Hatred of superiority and envy,
which have become the bane of democracy and threaten

its existence, derive from feelings too natural not to have existed always. But in the hierarchical societies of the past their display was difficult. Having free play today, and encouraged ceaselessly by politicians avid for popularity and by academic malcontents unhappy with their lot, these feelings now exert their disastrous tyranny. . . .

A society exists thanks to the maintenance of the hereditary conviction that it is necessary to respect religiously the laws on which the social organism is founded. . . .

To destroy belief in the necessity of respecting social restraints represented by laws is to prepare a revolution infinitely more dangerous than a material revolution. Pillaged monuments are rebuilt very fast, but to re-make the soul of a people often requires centuries. . . .

Of the revolutionary slogans reproduced on our money and on our walls, only equality impassions minds as it did. Fraternity is no longer discussed; the class struggle has become the slogan of our times. As for liberty, the crowd never understood its meaning and will always reject it. . . .

If education, tradition and law no longer are able to canalize people's impulses and consequent actions, they become prey not only to leaders but also to all the foreign enemies who know how to exploit them. . . .

We have seen that . . . there is a normal establish-ment among individuals of a kind of balance between their various impulses emanating from the logics that guide them and the same generally is true of peoples. . . . When, under certain influences, this balance is upset, profound perturbations occur and a revolution is imminent. The culmination of these is a mental illness resulting from the lack of balance between various impulses coming from several logics of which one has become too dominant.

It was the preponderance of mystical logic that produced the great upheavals of humanity. The Crusades, religious wars, the French Revolution furnish examples. . . . When affective logic predominates, one sees intense development of feelings expressed in warlike enterprises, or in their contrary, that is, the flourishing of humanitarianism and pacifism, of which the results are no less disastrous.

When rational logic seeks to intervene exclusively in the life of a people the upheavals are no less profound. Reason becomes a cloak dissimulating affective or mystical impulses.

In our times, crowds and their leaders . . . are as saturated with mysticism as in the days of our most remote ancestors. Words and formulae endowed with magical power have inherited the force once attributed to the divinities adored by our fathers. The hallucinating hope of paradise is always alive. . . .

The role of a great statesman is to know how to orient the destiny of people by using their affective and mystical impulses and by not trying to destroy them in the name of reason.

The conflicts among the diverse forms of logic are not continual. They tend . . . toward equilibrium.

The contradictions subsist but one finally arrives at scarcely noticing them. The intellectual elements often resign themselves to submission to affective and mystical influences without, however, admitting defeat. . . .

The ancient adage "know thyself" is happily impossible of realization, for if we knew ourselves, discovering the perpetual strife laying siege to our understanding, our existence would darken into a chaos of uncertainty. Not to know is sometimes better than to know. . . .

Affective truths, mystical truths and rational truths are daughters of logics too different ever to be fused. . . .

Too much affective logic leads one to give in without reflection to impulses which often are deadly. Too much mystical logic engenders a religious existence dominated by egotistical preoccupation with salvation and without social utility. To much collective logic enables inferior elements to predominate and leads them back to barbarism. Too much rational logic leads to doubt and inaction.

Part V

Individual Opinions and Beliefs

The ideal of a people determines a great number of its opinions and beliefs. It represents the synthesis of its common aspirations, of its needs and desires. This synthesis is determined by race, by the past, and many other factors . . . ; it cannot be shaken without disturbing the foundations of the society it sustains. If today so many men waver in their opinions and beliefs and obey the most contrary impulses, even if they are of very high intelligence, it is because they no longer have but a very weak ideal.

The power of fanatics lies precisely in that they obey rigorously their dangerous ideal. One can observe this today concerning the social ideal, the only one that still serves the multitudes. It weighs on all our national life and engenders a mass of laws injurious to our prosperity.

An ideal is therefore not at all a merely theoretical conception of which one can ignore the effect. Become general, it exercises a preponderant influence over the most insignificant details of life. Even those who ignore it are subject to its influence. Religious, moral and political beliefs attain power only after having been concretized in a universally accepted ideal. When it is adapted to the necessities and possibilities of the times, it determines the greatness of a nation. When it goes against the natural course of things, it provides decadence.

Part VI

Collective Opinions and Beliefs

The soul of a people is not a metaphysical conception but a very lively reality. It is composed of an atavistic stratification of traditions, ideas, ways of thinking, even prejudices. The strength of a nation depends on its solidity.

Men united simply through violent conquest constitute only a transitory aggregate not cemented and easily dissociated because they do not yet possess a national soul. For so long as it is not acquired, they remain but dust of barbarians. To destroy the influences of the past among a people always has had the invariable result of reducing them to barbarism.

Divergency of opinions among a people possessing a very strong national soul bears only on subjects of minor importance. When their greatest interest is affected, their accord becomes unanimous. . . .

The collective soul of a race shows itself only when considerable general interest is involved. It in no way impedes the existence of very lively individual souls, in the same way as in natural history the distinctive characteristics of each kind in a species do not prevent its having also those of the family to which it belongs.

We shall see that the elements constituting primitive races not yet differentiated have only a collective soul. It is only among highly evolved races that individual characteristics are superimposed on the collective characteristics. . . .

The formation of a soul in common is possible only among people of not too dissimilar origins. If the dissimilarities are too many, no fusion can take place.

Not possessing the same soul, each individual is impressed differently by exterior things and would not know, as a result, how to hold common opinions on any subject. The Czechs and Hungarians in Austria, the Irish in England are illustrations of the exactness of this law. The pretension of being able to impose our codes on natives in our colonies proves that it is little understood.

The mixing of very different races modifies their ancestral influences, but takes away at the same time their mental stability. A miscegenated people is ungovernable. The anarchy of the Latin American republics is the proof.

The mental heritage of the past stabilizes itself as a people grows old, and that which was its strength becomes in the end its weakness. Its adaptability to progress becomes more difficult, its thoughts and opinions become less and less free. There is a daily struggle between the consciousness that reason governs and the ancestral impulses which escape it. The violent revolutions by which peoples try sometimes to deliver themselves from the oppressive yoke of a too burdensome past destroys things but modifies their souls by only a very little. Thus the opinions and beliefs of old France put an irresistible weight on the new. Only the facades have changed.

The Influence of Social Milieu and Social Groups

The social milieu acts intensely on our opinions and conduct; it constantly engenders within us dominating unconscious inferences. Books, newspapers, discussions and the happenings of our epoch create an invisible ambience that orients us. They contain the sprouts of artistic, literary, scientific and philosophical concepts which genius sometimes condenses into luminous syntheses.

The opinions born of social milieu are so strong that the individual obliged to quit it is forced equally to alter his opinions. A perfect revolutionary socialist easily becomes a narrow conservative as soon as he has achieved power. One knows how easy it was for Napoleon to transform into dukes, court chamberlains and barons the fierce men of the [Revolutionary] Assembly who had not yet had the chance to cut off one another's heads.

Social milieu acts in a general way, but that which acts upon us most of all is the group to which we belong.

In general, we have very few opinions and beliefs deduced from reasoning based on experience and observation. Most men possess only those of the group: caste, class, sect, party or profession to which they belong and which they adopt in a bloc. . . .

He who does not adopt the opinions of the group to which he belongs can scarcely live in it. . . .

The present evolution toward socialism and syndicalism augments all groups, especially those administered by state monopolies. These are ferociously jealous of one another and have nothing in common except a torrent of enmities and disdain. There results a progressive disorganization among the services rendered by the state, which each day are becoming more numerous. . . .

The disagreements of opinion among groups of bureaucrats who, under the cloak of anonymity, are the real masters of the nation, are relatively unnoticed by the public. The opinions of workmen's groups are, on the contrary, too clamorous to be unobserved. Their hatred of other classes tends to become the most powerful factor of present day political evolution.

Under the influence of their leaders, they believe themselves to be the sole creators of wealth and grant no role to capital or intelligence. Believing themselves to be much more compatriots of foreign workers than of the French middle class, they have become internationalists and antimilitarists. Their true native land is the group of people in their trade no matter what country they belong to.

The Progressive Influence of Collective Opinions and the Consequences

The action of crowds becoming more and more considerable in political life lends great importance to the study of popular opinions. Interpreted by a legion of lawyers and professors, who transpose them and disguise their changeableness, incoherence and simplism, they remain nevertheless poorly known. Today the people as sovereign are as adored as were once upon a time the worst despots. Their base passions, clamorous appetites, their most unintelligent aspirations attract admirers. For politicians, servitors of the masses, no facts exist, realities have no worth, nature must adapt itself to all the fantasies of number. . . .

Perhaps the most important point about the psychology of crowds, I repeat, is the impotence of reason upon them. The ideas capable of influencing crowds are not rational ideas but feelings expressed in the form of ideas. . . .

The mystical side of the crowd soul is still more developed than its affective side. As a result there is an intense need to adore something—god, fetish, personage or doctrine.

This need extends itself today toward the socialist faith, a new religion of which the supernatural power is supposed to regenerate mankind. . . .

Among the characteristics of popular opinion one encounters two: mobility and stability, seemingly in contradictory aspect.

Mobility seems to be their law and it is, in effect; but like the ocean waves above the tranquil deep, this surface mobility conceals very stable elements. One discovers them beneath all the variations our history has offered during the last century.

Behind the constant mobility of the crowd, behind its furors, enthusiasms, violences and hates generating so much upheaval, there persist very tenacious conservative instincts. Even the most revolutionary Latin crowds remain very conservative, very traditional. That is why the regimes they overturn are soon replaced under different names.

This double tendency—revolutionary in actions, conservative in feelings—is generally overlooked by their leaders. . . .

The growing power of crowds being one of the inevitable factors of modern life, one must learn how to submit to it. Pascal already had resigned himself to it: "Why does one follow the majority? Is it because they are more correct? No; but more powerful." And by the very fact that power has been conferred on the majority, or on those who lead it, the majority are convinced that being all they can do all, therefore the flatterers of this new power increase every day in order to serve it. Legislators and ministers have become its slaves. . . .

The opinions of the crowd dictating today the laws that legislators enact, the final result is disorganization of the industrial, social and political life of the nation, since these laws correspond to ephemeral fantasies and not to necessities. As for governments, they are restricted to following the movements of opinion and, feeling powerless to direct them, they permit the accumulation of ruins. . . . They believe themselves to be voting for progress and liberty, whereas they are leading us into servitude and decadence and the despotisms which are their result. . . .

The destructive role of crowd opinions is, however, only one aspect of their action. Under the apparent popular mobility, as we have said, there is a traditional spirit rather difficult to destroy. Thanks to it crowds return easily to the past.

The conservative side of the popular soul is observed above all among social groups: classes, congresses, corporations, syndicates, academies, etc.

The action of these homogeneous groups often is very different from that of heterogeneous crowds. . . . Neither destructive nor creative, they stabilize, because of the authority of their number, the new opinions created by the elite and thus set for a certain time the important elements of a civilization: language, the arts, fashion, beliefs, even scientific theories.

Individual action certainly remains fundamental, and genius—its most beautiful flowering—always is personal; nevertheless its inventions cannot be fully enjoyed until after having become collective. Without solitary researchers, there never would have been either civilization or progress, but the work of an individual acquires full power only through its absorption by the collective soul.

Dissolution of the Individual Soul into the Collective Soul

After having been painfully disengaged through long secular effort from the collectivity, the individual soul is tending to return to it in an unexpected way much different from that imagined by certain political theoreticians dreaming of a general equalization of conditions and fortunes under the direction of the state.

Outside of socialist theories, and soon contrary to them, there are developing little groups clearly separated from one another in their opinions and interests. This disaggregation of society into fragments without common interests is what they call the trade union movement. Far from remaining purely theoretical and foreign to reality, like socialism, these groups are a spontaneous creation due to economic necessities imposed everywhere, as is proved by their ubiquity in diverse forms among people of entirely different mentalities. The only difference is that the trade union movement is revolutionary in some countries and pacifist in others.

The industrial revolution, which engendered this movement, led great modern nations to subdivide themselves into little ones respecting only their own laws and disdaining those of the general collective containing them.

The temporary union of these diverse groups, despite their different interests, endows them with quite a powerful force in making their will prevail. This force . . . will not last. As soon as the ancient social blocs have been entirely dissolved into solid little fragments, their divergent interests will lead them into fatally incessant struggles. If each group is in effect composed of homogeneous elements with identical interests and opinions, it will find itself in conflict with other groups just as powerful but with clearly opposite interests.

One can already foresee these future struggles between opposing interests in the example of the ancient Italian republics, notably those of Siena and Florence. Governed for centuries by trade unions, the cities of which they were masters were bloodied by their internecine struggles.

Let us not object that this was a matter of ancient times. The great social laws are not numerous and their effects always are repeated.

Today these struggles between groups are only beginning, because central government still has power and restrains their rivalries, but this power is more and more losing its effect. When it is disappearing, we shall see the conflict of these collective groups at first directed against the central power. . . .

Pillage, arson and massacres will then be, as was always the case, the inevitable manifestations of popular rage against the slightest resistance to their demands when there no longer are any brakes to hold them. . . .

The most important fact set forth in this chapter is the beginning of the disaggregation of present societies into little independent groups reciprocally hostile, seeking more and more to isolate themselves and robbing nations of their unity. The individual soul, which took centuries to disengage itself a little from the collective soul, actually is returning to it. Thus we are taking part in a strange phenomenon in which civilized peoples are tending toward the inferior mentality of the early primitive ages. The great struggles of the future will be less among different peoples than among groups set up in the heart of each of them.

The dissolution of the individual soul into the collective of a group does not constitute progress either for society or for the individual.

Part VII

The Propagation of Opinions and Beliefs

Affirmation and repetition are among the strong agents of the creation and propagation of opinions. Education is in part based on them. Politicians and leaders of all kinds make a daily practice of them. Affirmation and repetition are the principal substance of their speeches.

Affirmation does not need to be based on any rational proof whatsoever; it needs only to be brief, forceful and impressive. . . .

Repeated often enough, affirmation ends by creating first an opinion and later a belief.

Repetition is the essential complement to affirmation. To repeat a word, an idea, a formula often enough is to transform it inevitably into a belief. From the founder of a religion to the merchandiser of novelties, all men make use of repetition to persuade others.

Its power is so great that one ends by believing the

words and opinions one habitually expresses. Caesar never would attack Rome, the great Pompey kept on saying when the Senate implored him to take measures to defend it, and, as Montesquieu points out, "Because he had said it so many times, he kept on saying it." The conviction formed in Pompey's mind through these repetitions prevented his having recourse to methods which would have protected Rome and saved his own head, at least for a time. . . .

Treatises on logic describe in great detail the different elements that go into judgment. However, they overlook contagion and prestige. Yet these are precisely what determine the immense majority of our opinions.

At college they teach us that the principle of authority, a fundamental part of prestige, has been replaced by experience and observation, but the falsity of this assertion is easy to show.

Even leaving aside religious, political and moral opinions, in which reason never intervenes, and to consider only scientific opinions, one recognizes that they often have as sole basis of authority that which is announced and propagated by simple contagion. It could not be otherwise. The greater part of scientific experiments and observations is too complicated to be repeated, with the result that the word of the savant who announced them is believed. The authority of the master is as sovereign today as when Aristotle reigned. It is becoming even more omnipotent as science becomes more and more specialized.

Most of the opinions that education gives us have

only authority as basis, and we easily become accustomed to accepting without difficulty an opinion held by a personage crowned with prestige.

On the technical aspects of our professions we are capable of forming rather sound judgments. As for the rest, we do not even try to reason but prefer to accept, eyes shut, the opinions of a personage or group endowed with imposing prestige. In fact, one's destiny, whether one is a statesman, manager, artist, writer or scholar, depends above all on the amount of prestige possessed and, in consequence, the degree of unconscious suggestion that one can create. It is the mental domination that a man exercises which determines his success. That is why, sometimes, an absolute imbecile succeeds, because, not being conscious of his own stupidity, he never hesitates to assert his authority, and energetic, oft-repeated affirmation gains prestige. The most vulgar street hawker, strongly asserting the entirely imaginary superiority of his wares, exercises prestige amid the crowd surrounding him. . . .

Even among eminent scholars, prestige often is one of the surest factors of conviction. For ordinary minds, it always is. Prestige, creator of opinions and master of will, is a moral power superior to material powers. Societies are much more founded on it than on force. Returned almost alone from the Island of Elba, Napoleon, thanks to his prestige, reconquered France in a few days. Facing its aureole, the king's cannons remained silent and his armies faded away.

Mental Contagion

Mental contagion constitutes a psychological phenomenon of which the result is involuntary acceptance of certain opinions and beliefs. Its source is not conscious; it operates without any reasoning or reflection. It can be observed in all beings, human and animal, principally when they are in crowds. Its action is immense and it dominates all history.

Mental contagion represents, in effect, the essential element for the propagation of opinions and beliefs. Its force is often great enough to make an individual act against his own most evident interests. The story of countless martyrs, suicides, mutilations, etc., caused by mental contagion furnishes innumerable proofs.

All manifestations of psychic life can be contagious but it is the emotions in particular which propagate themselves in this manner. Contagious ideas are the syntheses of affective elements.

In everyday life, contagion may be limited by the inhibiting action of will, but given a cause of some kind—a violent change of milieu in times of revolution, or popular excitement, etc.—contagion easily exercises its influence and can transform peaceful individuals into bold warriors, placid bourgeois into cruel partisans. Under its influence the same individuals go from one political party to another and will exert as much energy in putting down a revolution as in fomenting it.

Mental contagion does not take place solely through direct contact among individuals. Books, newspapers, wire services, the most simple rumors can produce it. The more the means of communication are multiplied, the more people's will is reached and infected. Each day we are becoming more tied to those around us. Individual mentality is receding easily to its primitive collective form.

Fashion

The variations of sensibility under the changes of milieu, needs, preoccupations, etc., create a public spirit which varies from one generation to another and even sometimes several times within a generation. This public spirit, rapidly spread through mental contagion, determines what is called fashion. It is a powerful factor in dictating most of the elements of social life, and most of our opinions and beliefs.

Dress is not alone in being submitted to its dictates. The theater, literature, politics, the arts, even scientific ideas obey it and that is why certain works have a base of resemblance permitting one to speak of the style of an epoch.

Because of its unconscious action, one obeys fashion without being aware of it. Even the most independent minds are scarcely able to avoid it. It is not often that artists and writers dare to produce a work far distant from the ideas of the day.

Currents and Explosions of Opinion

Any opinion held universally constitutes a truth to the crowd.

An explosion of opinion is instant orientation in the same direction of violent emotions. . . .

Most modern revolutions break out in the form of an explosion. . . . By means of contagion, revolutionary movements spread quickly far beyond the classes of people directly interested. . . . A characteristic of revolutions is that they propagate themselves rapidly among classes which, far from having anything to gain by them, often have everything to lose. The middle classes—become socialist revolutionaries by simple contagion—would assuredly meet with total ruin if the movement of which they have become apostles were to triumph.

Happily, these explosions of popular opinion—very dangerous because reason has no effect on them—do not last very long.

Part VIII

The Life of Beliefs

The elements constituting our existence are attached . . . to three groups: organic life; affective life; intellectual life.

The need to believe belongs to affective life. It is as irreducible as hunger or love, and often is as imperious. . . .

Being an invincible need in our affective nature, belief cannot be voluntary and rational, any more than any other sentiment. Intelligence neither governs nor creates it.

Whatever his race or times, degree of ignorance or culture, man always has manifested the same thirst for belief. Belief appears to be mental food, as necessary to the life of spirit as material foods are to the physical body they sustain. The civilized man cannot do without it [belief] any more than the savage.

Descartes' universal doubt is a fiction of the mind. One sometimes goes through periods of skepticism, but one cannot dwell there. The philosopher doesn't believe in the same things as an ignorant man, but he accepts as few demonstrables. . . .

Knowledge instructs and there can be no civilization without it; but belief creates action. If it were necessary to wait to know before acting, inaction would be long lasting.

For centuries, beliefs were the only guide of humanity. They provided man with easy explanations of all problems, a daily guide of conduct. Temporary or ephemeral, beliefs constituted the great driving power of men's actions.

Religious beliefs form only a part of belief. The need to believe never was created by religions; on the contrary, it engenders religions. The divinities only furnish an object for our need to believe. As soon as man turns away from them, he plunges anew into some faith—chimerical politics, spells or fetishes.

The Intolerance of Beliefs

One of the most constant general characteristics of beliefs is their intolerance. The stronger the belief, the greater its intolerance. Men dominated by a certitude cannot tolerate those who do not accept it.

Verified through the ages, this law continues to be in effect today. One knows to what degree of religious furor believers arrive, both atheists and devotees. The wars of religion, the Inquisition, [the Massacre of] St. Bartholomew, the revocation of the Edict of Nantes, the [Reign of] Terror, the present persecutions of the clergy, etc., are examples.

The rare exceptions to this law are easy to explain. If the Romans accepted foreigners' divinities, it was that they formed for them a powerful hierarchy that one could seek to conciliate by worship.

Though animated by other principles, triumphant Buddhism was not persecuting. Teaching indifference to desire and considering gods and beings as empty illusions of no importance, it had no reason to be intolerant.

The modern sects of the goddess Reason are as intolerant and thirsty for sacrifice as their predecessors. . . .

Georges Sorel [a socialist] predicts very correctly that the first measure of triumphant socialism will be to massacre pitilessly all its adversaries. . . .

In matters of belief, intolerance and the violence which accompany it are not exclusively in the masses. They appear to be as developed, if not more so, in educated people and, besides, are more lasting. "I have sometimes marveled," wrote [Jules] Michelet, "at the ferocity of the literate. They arrive at excesses in their nervous furor that less cultivated men do not attain."

Independence of Opinions: The Social Role of Intolerance

Looked at solely from the point of reason, intolerance of belief seems intolerable. Practically, it is not so much so, because the need for independence permitting withdrawal from common belief is altogether exceptional. Servitude to social milieu circumscribes narrowly the limits of independence without one's complaining about it. Often, one doesn't even notice it. To become truly free, it would first be necessary to liberate oneself from the influence of social milieu and live in isolation.

Our maximum possible independence consists in sometimes putting forth a little resistance to the suggestions of our environment. The great majority do not oppose any at all, but follow the beliefs, opinions and prejudices of their group. They obey these with no more consciousness than autumn leaves blown by the wind.

It is only among a very limited elite that the faculty of having personal opinions is sometimes observed. All the progress of civilization is due to these superior minds, but one cannot wish their multiplication to be excessive. Unable to adapt to too rapid and deep progress, a society would quickly fall into anarchy. The necessary stability for its existence is established precisely because of a compact group of slow and mediocre minds governed by the influences of tradition and environment.

It is therefore useful for society to be composed of a majority of mediocre men desirous of behaving like everybody and keeping general opinions and beliefs as guides. It also is very useful that general opinion is intolerant, fear of criticism by others being one of the surest bases of our morale. Mediocrity of mind is thus a benefit for a people, above all when it is associated with certain traits of character. The English understood this instinctively and this is why their country is one of the most liberal in a world wherein free thoughts in general are quite poorly regarded. . . .

From transitory opinion, which is a simple sketch of a belief, to complete faith dominating all understanding, there are steps rarely scaled.

In certain epochs, however, they are. Then mystical impulses and the feelings born of them become so powerful that all social brakes, all repression and laws become incapable of putting a lock on them. It was

Polyeucte smashing the idols; it was the martyr defying
his torturers; it is the nihilist tossing a bomb into a
crowd with the chimerical hope of killing a principle.

When belief arrives at the stage of intensity, no dike
can hold it. It prevails over the most obvious interests,
the dearest feelings, and transforms into dazzling truths
the most glaring errors. No sacrifice becomes too great
for a believer wanting to propagate his faith. Like the
hypnotized patients studied by modern science, he lives
in a domain of pure hallucination.

Such exaltations generally are prepared by a previous period of anarchy during which old beliefs are
disaggregated and, as a result, so are the feelings they
support.

The mentality of martyrs of every kind is identical,
whether political, religious or social. Hypnotized by the
fixity of their dream, they joyfully sacrifice themselves
to assure the triumph of an idea without any hope of
recompense in this world or another. The history of
Russian terrorists and nihilists abounds with demon-
strable lessons on this point. It is not always hope of
heaven that makes martyrs.

The number of such hallucinated ones is happily not
very considerable in an epoch. Become too numerous,
they would overturn the world. Persecution of them is
powerless and only renders their example contagious. . . .

Let us consider the example of Viva Perpetua, worshipped by Christians as a saint. . . . The daughter of
a senator who thrice was consul and then president of

the Carthaginian Senate, this beautiful and wealthy patrician, secretly converted to Christianity, preferred to expose herself naked before the people and to be devoured alive by ferocious beasts rather than to make a show of burning a little incense on the altar of the emperor.

Believers consider such acts as proof of the power of their gods. Pure illusion, obviously, because there have been as many martyrs in all religions and all political sects. . . .

These facts and all those of the same order are very instructive. They prove the power of the mystical mind which is capable of triumphing over pain and dominating feelings considered to be the very basis of our existence. What could reason do against it?

Also, it is not with rational arguments that one can instigate crowds. With beliefs one can always dominate them. Powerful enough to struggle against nature and sometimes subdue it, reason does not have strength enough to edify beliefs and triumph over them.

Sometimes destructive, sometimes constructive, but always irresistible, beliefs constitute the most powerful force in history and are the real foundations of civilizations. People never survive for long the death of their gods.

The Certitudes Derived from Beliefs

A strong belief inspires certitudes that nothing can shake. From such certitudes derive most of the great historic events.

Muhammad was certain that God ordered him to found a new religion destined to regenerate the world, and he succeeded in overturning it. Peter the Hermit was certain that God wanted the tomb of Christ taken away from the infidels, and to reconquer it, millions of men died miserably. Luther was certain that the pope was Antichrist, that there was no purgatory and, in the name of truths of such order, Europe was put to the torch and bloodied for several centuries. The priests of the Inquisition were certain that God wanted to see the burning of heretics, and they depopulated Spain with their bonfires. Charles IX and Louis XIV were certain that the creator of the world could not tolerate the existence of Protestants, and to exterminate them, the former had recourse to [the Massacre of] St. Bartholomew and the latter to attack by mounted troops.

The [Revolutionary] Convention was certain that it was necessary to cut off a great number of heads to assure the happiness of mankind and, as a result, provoked wars and a dictatorship that led three million men to perish in Europe.

In our times, thousands of bourgeois filled with the certainty that socialism will regenerate the world, furiously demolish the last pillars upholding the society in which they live. . . .

Mystical and sentimental certitudes always are accompanied by the need to impose them on others.

Man gives in with difficulty, and as soon as he is strong enough never accepts that others do not share his certitudes. To impose them, he never will shrink away from the most raging tyranny or bloody slaughter.

The possessors of certitudes always have ravaged the world.

A belief is an act of faith not requiring proof and which, besides, almost always is not verifiable by any. If faith imposed itself only by rational argument, very few beliefs would have been formed during the course of the centuries. . . .

Since no rational elements take part in the genesis of faith, the credulity of the believer is infinite. . . .

The Age of Reason into which the progress of science has led humanity has in no way destroyed the power of beliefs or the ability to forge new ones. In no other epoch, perhaps, has one seen so many blossom —political, religious or social. America and Russia, notably, give birth to new ones each day. . . .

A belief, whether political, religious, artistic or moral, has in reality nothing stable except its name. It is an organism in the process of incessant evolution. I have already explained in the *Psychology of the Evolution of Peoples* how institutions, languages, beliefs and the arts are transformed. I showed that these elements never can pass from one people to another without undergoing considerable modification. . . .

The laws ruling the evolution of beliefs are far from being clearly determined. Yet one can formulate, I think, the following indications:

(1) Several reconcilable beliefs when set forth tend

toward fusion, or at least, toward superimposition. This occurred concerning the gods and beliefs of the pagan world.

(2) If beliefs are very different, the strongest—which often signifies the simplest—tends to diminish the others. Thus Islamism converted not only savage tribes in Africa but also very civilized people in India.

(3) A triumphant belief always ends by dividing itself into sects, each preserving only the most fundamental elements of the mother faith. . . .

The division of a belief into sects always has been favored by the extreme imprecision of its sacred books. Each theologian can interpret them according to his taste. . . .

The disaggregation of a belief into rival sects, perpetually in strife with one another, did not occur in polytheistic religions. They too went through an evolution, but by simple annexation and fusion of new gods, all considered as very powerful and therefore respected. That is why the wars of religion which ravaged Europe were almost unknown in pagan antiquity.

Thus it was a great benefit for peoples to have begun with polytheism. I believe, contrary to almost universal opinion, that peoples might have gained much by remaining polytheistic. Far from favoring progress, monotheism retarded it by the bloody struggles with which it filled the world. It slowed for centuries the evolution of the art, philosophy and literature developed by the Greek polytheists to such a stage that we regard them as our teachers.

One cannot consider as an advantage the unity of sentiments which monotheism ended by creating by means of wars, burnings at the stake and proscriptions. The cult of nationhood was enough to endow the polytheistic Romans, in their time of greatness, with a community of sentiment that never has been surpassed. . . .

The changes of faith . . . have a great historical importance because of the role they played; but from the point of view of philosophy they are without interest. Faith constitutes food demanded by our need to believe. The food has changed and will be changed again, but the need will remain indestructible for so long as human nature has not been changed.

How Faiths Die

Correct in the historical sense, the title of this chapter is much less so in the philosophical sense. Similar to energy in modern physics, faiths sometimes are transformed but never die. They change their name, nevertheless, and it is this phenomenon that perhaps can be considered to be their death. Thus, after having slowly grown old, dogmas obey natural law. They become blurred and then die away. Their disappearance, or rather their transformation, first goes through a critical phase, often the generator of upheavals.

Physicists have shown that when a body approaches its critical point, even an insignificant variation in temperature abruptly forces it to pass from a gaseous to a liquid state, or inversely. This critical point is observed equally in many social phenomena. . . . The phenomenon, so general in physics or political economy, is also manifested in the life of beliefs. After many oscillations and prolonged usage, they sometimes arrive at a critical point and are abruptly changed.

This phase, where skepticism and faith are side by side, occurs when the passage of time or other incentives have unsettled beliefs before those that will replace them are clearly formulated.

The last defenders of disintegrating dogmas hold on to them despairingly without very much believing in them. "They seem to fear that incurable boredom," said [Jacques] Bossuet, "which is the essence of life since they lost their taste for God."

Actually, they never lost it; new gods always replace those which are dead or will die. But the passage from one divinity to another always entails great difficulties. This can be shown, for example, upon the decline of paganism.

We are now going through precisely one of those ages of instability in which people find themselves torn by the influences of ancient gods and those in process of being created. Our epoch constitutes a critical point in the history of beliefs.

While awaiting the adoption of a great new faith, the popular soul floats between little momentary dogmas of no lasting duration but nonetheless not without force. Defended by groups, committees, parties, they exercise considerable power. Examples are the action of clubs during the Revolution, the trade unions among the working classes, the electoral committees in little towns.

Though seemingly ephemeral, these little beliefs engender during their existence a robust faith. The irresistible need to believe . . . is concentrated on them. Nevertheless, they cannot replace definitively the general beliefs. Though the chapters of these groups are in an incessant rivalry, the great dogmas have the power to force individual interests to give way to collective interests.

It is obvious that we are not at such a stage today. The great general categorical imperatives have become the little imperatives of sects having nothing in common except an intense hatred of order and of the establishment. The tables of law are no longer the same for all the tribes of Israel.

Transformation of Religious Faith into Political Faith

Examined briefly, our modern age seems to have transposed all scales of value. In reality, it has only modified their names.

The faithful of old cults lament the lack of faith of the new generation. Perhaps never before, however, have the crowds shown a more profound need to believe than in our epoch. In becoming political faith, religious faith has not changed very much. Belief in miracles, the mystical adoration of supernatural powers have remained identical. Statist Providence has inherited Divine Providence. . . .

Our epoch, I cannot repeat this too often, can be understood only by grasping the role played by the mysticism of the people and their leaders. . . .

I have shown in preceding works the evolution of socialism toward a religious form. . . . If it possessed a definite divinity to adore, its success would be much more rapid. . . .

Abstract divinities never have seduced the crowd and that is why the socialist réligion has its dogmas but still awaits its god. He will not be too long in coming. Gods always are born when the need for them makes itself felt. . . .

Belief is an irresistible master and its attraction is exercised the moment one approaches the sphere of action.

Tenacious or transitory, beliefs represent, I repeat again, the great factors in the life of nations. One cannot govern a people with true ideas but only with beliefs accepted as truths.

Part IX

The Intervention of Belief in the Cycle of Knowledge: The Genesis of Scientific Illusions

No scholar can boast of having quit for always the cycle of belief. He is obliged to formulate theories and hypotheses in incompletely known phenomena, that is to say, beliefs for which only the authority of their authors can win acceptance. . . .

Experience and observation are the only support of true certainty. The impossibility of certifying the whole of our knowledge renders illusory the advice given by Descartes in his "Discourse on Method": "Never accept as true anything that I do not know certainly as such, and reject as false all those things about which we can imagine the slightest doubt."

If Descartes had applied his precepts, he would not have accepted things as certain which are laughable to us today. Like all his contemporaries and his successors in general, he was dominated by belief. Even the most intense skepticism is in reality always partial. "He who is willing to accept nothing in the ordinary affairs of life that is not founded on clear and direct proof, could assure himself of nothing except to perish within a short time," says Locke. "He could not find any food or drink with which he would dare to nourish himself."

One can add that critical analysis of our opinions and our certitudes would render existence in society impossible. The role of belief is precisely to avoid such analyses for us. And since the scholar is obliged to accept as beliefs a great part of the truths of science, it is not surprising to see him display sometimes as much credulity as ignorant people. On subjects outside his specialty, sometimes he even outdoes them.

The Modern Form of Belief in Occultism

Man always has thirsted to know his destiny and obtain the aid of supernatural powers he believes surround him. From these needs were born all forms of belief in magic.

This art has been practiced by all peoples in all the ages of history. Necromancy, astrology, and soothsaying, branches of magic, have been in constant usage since antiquity. . . .

One sees the role of mental suggestion and contagion in the supernatural phenomena attached to magic and their influence on the most eminent minds. . . .

But this analysis is not sufficient. To understand the genesis of practices which have persisted among all peoples in all ages, and which still exist, it is necessary to arrive at a more general concept and not to try to explain by means of reason that which does not belong to it.

Magic, in all its forms, should be considered as a manifestation of a mystical spirit inseparable from our nature. . . .

Founders of religions, sorcerers, magicians, soothsayers—propagators of so many illusions which have charmed or terrorized our fathers and always reappear—are the priests of a powerful goddess who rules all others and whose cult appears to be eternal. . . .

One discovers her by inquiring into what it was that so many men hoped to find in the various gods they invoked. One single sentiment always visibly inspired them. People of all races adore, under various names, only one divinity: Hope. All their gods were therefore only a single God.

Conclusions

One of the fundamental problems indicated at the beginning of this work was to study how beliefs which no rational argument could defend always have been accepted without difficulty by even the most enlightened minds of all ages.

For so long as psychology regarded belief as voluntary and rational, the study of such a problem could not be undertaken. To dissociate the generating elements of belief, to prove that it is unconscious and formed under the influence of mystical and affective elements independent of reason and will was to indicate the broad lines of the sought-after solution. But this explanation remains incomplete. If reason doesn't create beliefs, it can at least discuss them and discover in them their erroneous aspects. Why, nevertheless, despite the clearest proofs, does a belief succeed in imposing itself?

We explained this by proving the fundamental role exercised on the unconscious by certain factors: prestige, affirmation, repetition, suggestion and contagion. Independent of reason, these act against it and prevent the recognition of evidence.

The power of these influences on the genesis of beliefs is proved by their effects on the actions of even the most cultivated men. . . .

The only real difference between a scientific belief . . . and religious, political or spiritual belief . . . is that in a scientific matter error is eliminated fairly quickly through the substitution of belief by knowledge. Since certainty based on affective or mystical elements involves elements in which no immediate verification is possible, observation, reason, even experience remain on the contrary almost without effect.

I have, I hope, put into evidence a mental mechanism which up to now psychological research has left unexplained.

We have arrived thus at this important philosophical law: Far from presenting a common intellectual origin, our concepts have very different mental sources and are ruled by very different forms of logic. From the predominance of each and their conflicts are born the great happenings of history.

While waiting for science to reveal the immutable truths, hidden perhaps behind the appearances of things, we must be content with the certainties accessible to our minds.

In the actual state of knowledge, three orders of truths guide us: affective truths, mystical truths, and rational truths. Born of different logics, they have no common measure.

Part VI

The Psychology of Revolutions

(La Psychologie des Révolutions)

First edition published in Paris by E. Flammarion, 1912. First published in English in the United States by G. P. Putnam's Sons, New York, 1913; reprinted by Fraser Publishing Company, Wells, Vermont, 1968.

Tocqueville has no difficulty in proving that the [French] Revolution [of 1789] did little but overturn that which was about to fall.

If in reality the Revolution destroyed but little, it favored the fruition of certain ideas which continued to develop thereafter. The fraternity and liberty which it proclaimed never greatly seduced the people, but equality became their gospel—the pivot of socialism and of the entire evolution of modern democratic ideas.

The Classification of Revolutions

We generally apply the term *revolution* to sudden political changes, but the expression may be employed to denote all sudden transformations, or apparently sudden, whether of beliefs, ideas or doctrines. . . .

A revolution may finally become a belief, but it often begins under the action of perfectly rational motives—

the suppression of crying abuses, of a detested despotic government, or an unpopular sovereign, etc.

Although the origin of a revolution may be perfectly rational, we must not forget that the reasons invoked in preparing for it do not influence the crowd until they have been transformed into sentiments. Rational logic can point to the abuses to be destroyed, but to move the multitude its hopes must be awakened. . . .

The multitude is . . . the agent of a revolution but not its point of departure. The crowd represents an amorphous being which can do nothing and will do nothing without a head to lead it. It will quickly exceed the impulse received but never creates it.

The sudden political revolutions which strike the historian most forcibly are often the least important. The great revolutions are those of manners and thought. Changing the name of a government does not transform the mentality of a people. To overthrow the institutions of a people is not to reshape its soul.

The true revolutions, those which transform the destinies of peoples, are most frequently accomplished so slowly that the historian can hardly point to their beginnings. The term *evolution* is therefore far more appropriate than *revolution*.

We will divide [the majority of revolutions] into scientific revolutions, political revolutions and religious revolutions.

Scientific revolutions are by far the most important. Although they attract but little attention, they often are fraught with remote consequences such as are not engendered by political revolutions. . . .

These scientific revolutions in the domain of ideas are purely intellectual. Our sentiments and beliefs do not affect them. Men submit to them without discussing them. Their results being controllable by experience, they escape all criticism. . . .

Beneath and very remote from these scientific revolutions, which generate the progress of civilization, are the religious and political revolutions, which have no kinship with them. While scientific revolutions derive solely from rational elements, political and religious beliefs are sustained exclusively by affective and mystic factors. Reason plays only a feeble part in their genesis. . . .

By the very fact that it is regarded as an absolute truth, a belief necessarily becomes intolerant. This explains the violence, hatred and persecution which were the habitual accompaniments of the great political and religious revolutions, notably of the Reformation and the French Revolution. . . .

It is obvious that revolutions never have taken place and never will take place except with the aid of an important fraction of the army. Royalty did not disappear in France on the day when Louis XVI was guillotined, but at the precise moment when his mutinous troops refused to defend him. . . .

A military movement may overthrow a government —and in the Spanish republics the government is

hardly ever destroyed by any other means—but if the
revolution is to be productive of great results it must
always be based upon general discontent and general
hopes.

Unless it is universal and excessive, discontent alone
is not sufficient to bring about a revolution. It is easy
to lead a handful of men to pillage, destroy and massacre, but to raise a whole people or any great portion of
that people calls for the continuous and repeated action
of leaders. These exaggerate the discontent; they persuade the discontented that the government is the sole
cause of all their troubles, especially of a prevailing
dearth, and assure men that the proposed new system
will engender an age of happiness. These ideas germinate, propagating themselves by suggestion and contagion, and the moment arrives when the revolution is
ripe. . . .

In religious revolutions, no experience can reveal to
the faithful that they are deceived, since they would
have to go to heaven to make the discovery. In political
revolutions, experience quickly demonstrates the error
of a false doctrine and forces men to abandon it. Thus
at the end of the Directorate [in the French Revolution]
the application of Jacobin beliefs had led France to
such a degree of ruin, poverty and despair that the
wildest Jacobins themselves had to renounce their own
system. Nothing survived of their theories except a few
principles unable to be verified by experience, such as

the universal happiness that equality would bestow upon humanity.

The Reformation was finally to exercise a profound influence upon the sentiments and moral ideas of a great proportion of mankind. Modest in its beginnings, it was at first a simple struggle against the abuses of the clergy and, from a practical point of view, a return to . . . the Gospel. It never constituted, as has been claimed, an aspiration toward freedom of thought. Calvin was as intolerant as Robespierre. . . . Indeed, in every country where the Reformation was established the sovereign replaced the pope of Rome with the same rights and the same powers. . . .

Luther having taught that the clergy had no need of wealth, the German lords found many merits in a faith which enabled them to seize the goods of the church. Henry VIII enriched himself by a similar operation. Sovereigns who were often molested by the pope could as a rule only look favorably upon a doctrine which added religious powers to their political ones and made each of them a pope. Far from diminishing the absolutism of rulers, the Reformation only exaggerated it.

The Reformation overturned all Europe and came near to ruining France, of which it made a battlefield for a period of fifty years. Never did a cause so insignificant from the rational point of view produce such momentous results. . . .

I have already stated that intolerance always is an

accompaniment of powerful religious beliefs. Political and religious revolutions furnish us with innumerable proofs of this fact, and show us also that the mutual intolerance of sects of the same religion is always much greater than that of defenders among remote and alien faiths, such as Islamism and Christianity. . . . Catholics and Protestants adored exactly the same God and only differed in their manner of adoring Him. . . .

Reason being powerless to affect the mind of the convinced, Protestants and Catholics continued their ferocious conflicts. All the efforts of their sovereigns to reconcile them were in vain. . . . In all history, no one can cite an example of a belief destroyed or reduced by means of refutation. Catherine [de Medicis] did not even know that although toleration is with difficulty possible between individuals, it is impossible between collectivities. . . .

We must not hope to see peoples possessed by strong beliefs readily achieve tolerance. The only people who attained toleration in the ancient world were the poly-theists. The nations practicing toleration at the present time are those which might as well be described as polytheistical, since, as in England and America, they are divided into innumerable sects. Under identical names they really adore very different deities.

The multiplicity of beliefs which results in such toleration finally results also in weakness. We therefore arrive at a psychological problem not yet resolved: how to have a faith that is both powerful and tolerant. . . .

Despite their slight rational value, they [religious revolutions and beliefs] shape history and prevent the peoples from remaining a mass of individuals without cohesion of strength. Man has needed them at all times to orient his thought and guide his conduct. No philosophy has as yet succeeded in replacing them.

The Action of Governments in Revolutions

Governments almost invariably fight against revolutions; they hardly ever create them. Representing needs of the moment and general opinion, they [governments] follow the reformers timidly but do not precede them. Sometimes, however, certain governments have attempted those sudden reforms known as revolutions. The stability or instability of the national mind decrees the success or failure of such attempts.

They succeed when the people on whom the government seeks to impose new institutions is composed of semibarbarous tribes without fixed laws and without solid traditions, that is, without a settled national mind. Such was the condition of Russia in the days of Peter the Great. We know how he sought to Europeanize the semi-Asiatic populations by means of force.

Japan is another example of a revolution affected by government. But it was her machinery not her mind that was reformed.

It requires a very powerful autocrat aided by a man of genius to succeed even partially in such a task. [That

of a government-created revolution.] More often than
not the reformer finds that the whole people rise up
against him. Then, to the contrary of what occurs in an
ordinary revolution, the autocrat is revolutionary and
the people are conservative. . . . Attentive study will
show that the peoples always are extremely conservative.

Failure is the rule with these attempts. Whether
effected by the upper or lower classes, revolutions do
not change the soul of peoples that have been established for a long time. They change only those things
that are worn out by time and ready to fall.

China is at present making a very interesting but impossible experiment in seeking, by means of government, to renew the institutions of the country. The
revolution which overturned the dynasty of her ancient
sovereigns was the indirect consequence of the discontent provoked by reforms which the government
had sought to impose with a view toward ameliorating
the condition of China. The suppression of opium and
gambling, the reform of the army, and the creation of
schools involved an increase in taxation which, as well
as the reforms themselves, greatly upset popular
opinion.

A few cultivated Chinese educated in European
schools profited by this discontent to rally the people
and proclaim a republic, an institution about which the
Chinese could have had no conception. It surely cannot
long survive, for the impulse which gave birth to it is

not a movement of progress but of reaction. To the Chinese intellectualized by his European education, the word *republic* is simply synonymous with rejection of the yoke of laws, rules and long-established restraints. Cutting off his pigtail, covering his head with a cap and calling himself a Republican, the young Chinese thinks he can give free rein to all his instincts. This is more or less the idea of a republic that a large part of the French people entertained at the time of the great Revolution.

China will soon discover the fate that awaits a society deprived of the armor slowly wrought by the past. After a few years of bloody anarchy it will be necessary to establish a power whose tyranny will inevitably be far more severe than that which was overthrown. Science has not yet discovered the magic wand capable of saving a society without discipline. There is no need to impose discipline when it has become hereditary; but when the primitive instincts are allowed to destroy the barriers painfully erected by slow ancestral labors, they cannot be reconstituted except by an energetic tyranny. . . .

If we knew nothing of France except the disturbances of the last hundred years and more, we might suppose the country to live in a state of profound anarchy. On the contrary, her economic, industrial and even her political life manifest a continuity which seems to be independent of all revolutions and governments.

The fact is that besides the great events, with which history deals, are the little facts of daily life that books do not tell us about. These are ruled by imperious necessities which halt for no man. Their total mass forms the real framework of the life of a people. . . .

Who, in truth, are the real rulers of a people? Kings and ministers, no doubt, in the great crises of national life, but they play no part whatever in the little realities making up everyday life. The real directing forces of a country are the administrations composed of impersonal elements which never are affected by changes of government. Conservative in traditions, they are anonymous and lasting, and constitute an occult power before which all other powers must eventually bow. Their action has even increased to such a degree that, as we shall presently show, there is a danger that they may form an anonymous state more powerful than the official state. France has thus come to be governed by heads of departments and government clerks. The more we study the history of revolutions, the more we discover that they change practically nothing but the label. To create a revolution is easy, but to change the soul of a people is difficult indeed.

The Part Played by the People in Revolutions

The aggregation of thoughts, sentiments, traditions and prejudices constituting the national mind built up by slow accumulations in the past during centuries makes the strength of a race. Without it no progress is possible. Each generation would require a fresh beginning.

The aggregate composing the soul of a people is solidly established only if it possesses a certain rigidity, but this rigidity must not go beyond a certain limit or there would be no such thing as malleability. Without rigidity the ancestral soul would have no stability, and without malleability it could not adapt itself to the changes of environment resulting from the progress of civilization. Excessive malleability of the national mind impels a people to incessant revolutions. Excess of rigidity leads it to decadence. . . .

Few peoples have succeeded in effecting the correct balance between these two contrary qualities of stability and malleability. The Romans in antiquity and the English in modern times may be cited among those who have best attained it.

The peoples whose mind is most fixed and established often effect the most violent revolutions. Not having succeeded in evolving progressively, in adapting themselves to changes of environment, they are forced to adapt themselves violently when such adaptation becomes indispensable.

Stability is acquired only very slowly. The history of a race is above all the story of its long efforts to establish its mind. So long as it has not succeeded it forms a horde of barbarians without cohesion and strength. After the invasions of the end of the Roman Empire, France took several centuries to form a national soul. She finally achieved one; but in the course of centuries this soul finally became too rigid. With a little more malleability, the ancient monarchy would have been slowly transformed as it was elsewhere and we should have avoided, together with the Revolution and its consequences, the heavy task of remaking a national soul.

The preceding considerations show us the part of race in the genesis of revolutions, and explain why the same revolutions will produce such different effects in different countries; why, for example, the ideas of the French Revolution, welcomed with such enthusiasm by some peoples, were rejected by others.

Certainly, England—though a very stable country —has suffered two revolutions and slain a king; but the mold of her mental armor was at once stable enough to retain the acquisitions of the past and malleable enough to modify them only within the necessary limits. Never did England dream, as did the men of the French Revolution, of destroying the ancestral heritage in order to erect a new society in the name of reason. . . .

The influence of race in the destiny of peoples appears plainly in the history of the perpetual revolutions of the Spanish republics in South America. Composed of . . . individuals whose diverse heredities have dissociated their ancestral characteristics, these populations have no national soul and therefore no stability. A people of half-castes is always ungovernable.

If we would learn more of the differences of political capacity which the racial factor creates, we must examine the same nation governed by two races successively. . . . This has been manifested in a striking manner . . . in Cuba and the Philippines which passed suddenly from Spanish rule to that of the United States.

We know in what anarchy and poverty Cuba existed under Spanish rule; we know too to what a degree of prosperity the island was brought within a few years after it fell under the influence of the United States.

The same experience was repeated in the Philippines, which for centuries had been governed by Spain. Finally the country was no more than a vast jungle, the home of epidemics of every kind. After a few years of American rule, the country was entirely transformed; malaria, yellow fever, plague and cholera had entirely disappeared. The swamps were drained; the country was covered with railways, factories and schools. In thirteen years, the mortality rate was reduced by two-thirds.

It is to such examples that we must refer the theorist who has not yet grasped the profound significance of the word *race,* and how far the ancestral soul of a people rules over its destiny.

How the People Regard Revolution

The part of the people has been the same in all revolutions. It is never the people who conceive or direct them. Their activity is released by means of leaders. . . .

The laws of psychology of crowds show us that the people never act without leaders, and that although they play a considerable part in revolutions by following and exaggerating the impulses received, they never direct their own movements.

In all political revolutions we discover the action of leaders. They do not create the ideas serving as the basis of revolutions but they use them as a means of action. Ideas, leaders, armies and crowds constitute four elements all having their part to play in revolutions.

The crowd, aroused by the leaders, acts especially by means of its mass. Its action is comparable to that of the shell which perforates an armor plate by the momentum of a force it did not create. Rarely does the crowd understand anything of the revolutions accomplished with its assistance. It obediently follows its leaders without even trying to find out what they want. . . .

In order to correspond with certain theoretical concepts, the people were formed into a mystic entity endowed with all powers and virtues, and praised incessantly by politicians overwhelming them with flattery. . . .

To the Jacobins of this epoch [the French Revolution], as well as to those of our times, this popular entity constitutes a superior personality possessing attributes peculiar to the gods of never having to answer for their actions and never making a mistake. Their wishes must be humbly acceded to. The people may kill, burn, ravage, commit the most frightful cruelties, glorify their hero today and throw him into the gutter tomorrow, it is all the same; the politicians will not cease to vaunt the people's virtues and to bow to their every decision.

Now in what really does this entity, the people, consist, this mysterious fetish revered by revolutionaries for more than a century?

The people may be broken down into two distinct categories. The first category includes the peasants, traders and workers of all sorts who need tranquility and order that they may exercise their calling. These form a majority, but a majority who never cause a revolution. Living in laborious silence, they are ignored by historians.

The second category, which plays a major part in all national disturbances, consists of a subversive social residue dominated by a criminal mentality. Degenerates of alcoholism and poverty, thieves, beggars, destitute drifters, apathetic unemployed workers—these constitute the dangerous bulk of the armies of insurrection. Fear of punishment prevents many of them from becoming criminals at ordinary times, but they do become criminals as soon as they can exercise their evil instincts without danger.

To this sinister substratum are due the massacres which stain all revolutions. . . . It was this class which, guided by its leaders, continually invaded the great revolutionary Assemblies. These regiments of disorder had no other ideal than that of massacre, pillage and incendiarism. Their indifference to theories and principles was complete.

To the elements recruited from the lowest dregs of the populace are added, by way of contagion, a host of idle and apathetic persons who are simply drawn into the movement. They shout because there is a revolt, without having the vaguest idea of the cause of shouting or of revolution. The suggestive power of their environment absolutely hypnotizes them and impels them to action.

These noisy and maleficent crowds, the kernel of all insurrections from antiquity to our own times, are the only crowds known to the orator. To him they are the sovereign people. . . .

At no period of history was the role of the lowest elements of the population exercised in such a lasting way as in the French Revolution. . . .

It was really a religion that the bourgeois of the first assembly thought to found. They thought to have destroyed an old world and built a new one on its ruins. Never did more seductive illusions fire the hearts of men. Equality and fraternity, proclaimed by the new dogmas, were to bring the reign of eternal happiness to all peoples. Man had broken forever with a past of barbarity and darkness. The regenerating world would be illumined in the future by the lucid radiance of pure reason. . . .

That this enthusiasm was so soon replaced by violence was due to the fact that the awakening was speedy and terrible. One can readily conceive of the indignant fury with which the apostles of the revolution attacked the daily obstacles opposed to the realization of their dreams. They had sought to replace the past, to forget tradition, to make man over again. But the past reappeared incessantly and men refused to change. The reformers, checked in their onward march, would not give in. They sought to impose by force a dictatorship which speedily made men regret the system abolished and finally led to its return.

The Revolutionary Mentality

In all ages, societies have contained a certain number of restless, unstable and discontented spirits ready to rebel against any established order of affairs. They are actuated by mere love of revolt and if some magic power could fulfill all their desires they would simply revolt again. This special mentality often results from a faulty adaptation of the individual to his surroundings, or from an excess of mysticism, but it may also be merely a question of temperament or arise from pathological disturbances.

The need of revolt presents very different degrees of intensity, from simple discontent expressed in words directed against men and things to the need of destroying them. Sometimes the individual turns upon himself the revolutionary frenzy that he cannot otherwise exercise. Russia is full of these madmen who, not content with committing arson or hurling bombs at hazard into the crowd, finally mutilate themselves, like the Skopzi and other analogous sects.

These perpetual rebels are generally highly suggestible human beings whose mystic mentality is obsessed by fixed ideas. Despite the apparent energy indicated by their actions, they really are weak characters and are incapable of mastering themselves sufficiently to resist the impulses that rule them. The mystic spirit which animates them furnishes pretexts for their violence and enables them to regard themselves as great reformers.

In normal times, the rebels which every society contains are restrained by . . . all the usual social constraints and therefore remain undetected. But as soon as a time of disturbance begins, these constraints grow weaker and the rebel can give free rein to his instincts. He then becomes the accredited leader of a movement. The motive of the revolution matters little to him; he will give his life indifferently for the red flag or white, or for the liberation of a country which he has heard vaguely mentioned.

This revolutionary spirit is not always pushed to the extremes which render it dangerous. When it has an intellectual origin, instead of being derived from affective or mystic impulses, it may become a source of progress. It is thanks to those spirits who are sufficiently independent to be intellectually revolutionary that a civilization is able to escape from the yoke of tradition and habit when these become too heavy. The sciences, arts and industries especially have progressed through the aid of such men. Galileo, Lavoisier, Darwin, and Pasteur were such revolutionaries. Although it is not necessary that a nation should possess any large number of such spirits, it is very necessary that it should possess some. Without them men would still be living in caves.

The revolutionary audacity which results in discoveries implies very rare faculties. It necessitates notably an independence of mind sufficient to escape from the influence of current opinions, and a judgment that can grasp, underneath superficial analogies, the hidden realities. This form of revolutionary spirit is creative, while that previously examined is destructive. The revolutionary mentality may therefore be compared to certain physiological states in the life of the individual which are normally useful but which, when exaggerated, take a pathological form which always is hurtful. . . .

All civilized societies inevitably drag behind them a residue of degenerates, of unadapted persons affected by various taints. . . . In ordinary times these waste products of civilization are more or less restrained by the police. During revolution nothing restrains them and they can easily gratify their instincts to murder and plunder. The revolutionaries of all times are sure of finding recruits in the dregs of society. . . .

To these criminals . . . the incurable plagues of all societies, we must add the class of semicriminals. Wrongdoers on occasion, they never rebel so long as fear of the established order restrains them, but as soon as it weakens they enroll themselves in the army of the revolution.

These two categories—habitual and occasional criminals—form an army of disorder which is fit for nothing except creation of disorder. All the revolutionaries, all founders of religious or political leagues, have constantly counted on their support. . . .

Traditions and Revolutionary Principles

The modern state, whoever its leader, has inherited in the eyes of the multitudes and their leaders the mystic power attributed to ancient kings when these latter were regarded as an incarnation of the divine will. Not only the people are inspired by this confidence in the power of government but also our legislators.

Always legislating, politicians never realize that as institutions are effects not causes, they have no virtue in themselves. Heirs to the great revolutionary illusion, they do not see that man is created by a past whose foundations we are powerless to shape. . . .

A tyrant can be overthrown; but what can be done against a host of little anonymous tyrannies?

If we wished to sum up in a word the great transformation which has been effected in France by a century of riots and revolutions, we might say that individual tyranny, which was weak and therefore easily overthrown, has been replaced by collective tyrannies which are very strong and difficult to destroy. To a people avid for equality and accustomed to hold its government responsible for every event, individual tyranny seemed insupportable, while a collective tyranny is readily endured although generally much more severe.

The extension of the tyranny of the state has therefore been the final result of all our revolutions, and the common characteristic of all systems of government we have known in France. This form of tyranny may be regarded as a racial ideal, since successive upheavals in France have only fortified it. Statism is the real political system of the Latin peoples and the only system that receives all votes. The other forms of government—republic, monarchy, empire—represent empty labels, powerless shadows.

The Recent Evolution of the Revolutionary Principles

Although the life of the Revolution [of 1789] was short, the influence of its principles was, on the contrary, very long-lived. Becoming a form of religious belief, they profoundly modified the orientation of the feelings and ideas of several generations. . . .

The heritage of the Revolution is summed up in the one phrase: liberty, equality and fraternity. . . . But while liberty has become very doubtful and fraternity has completely vanished, the principle of equality has grown unchecked. . . . It constitutes the real legacy of the Revolution. The craving for equality, not only before the law but also in position and fortune, is the very pivot of the end-product of democracy: socialism. This craving is so powerful it is spreading in all directions, although in contradiction to all biological and economic laws. It is a new phase of the continual struggle between feelings and reason in which reason so rarely triumphs.

The Democracy of the "Intellectuals" and Popular Democracy

All ideas that have hitherto caused an upheaval in the world of men have been subject to two laws: they evolve slowly; they change their sense completely according to the mentalities in which they find reception. . . .

Modified rapidly by men of different mentalities, the original theory is soon no more than a label denoting something quite unlike itself.

Applicable to religious beliefs, these principles are equally so to political beliefs. When a man speaks of democracy, for example, we must inquire what this word means to various peoples, and also whether in the same people there is not a great difference between the democracy of the "intellectuals" and popular democracy. . . .

The democracy of the lettered classes has no other aim than to set up a selection to recruit the ruling classes exclusively from among themselves. I should have nothing to say against this if the selection were real. It would then constitute the application of Napoleon's maxim: "The true method of government is to employ aristocracy, but under the forms of democracy."

Unhappily, the democracy of the "intellectuals" would simply lead to the substitution of the Divine right of kings by the Divine right of a petty oligarchy which is too often narrow and tyrannical. Liberty cannot be created by replacing a tyranny.

Popular democracy by no means aims at manufacturing rulers. Dominated entirely by the spirit of equality and the desire to ameliorate the lot of the workers, it rejects the idea of fraternity and exhibits no concern in respect of liberty. No government is conceivable to popular democracy except in the form of an autocracy. We see this not only in history, which shows us that since the Revolution all despotic governments have been vigorously acclaimed, but also in the autocratic fashion in which the workers' trade unions are conducted.

This profound distinction between the democracy of the lettered classes and popular democracy is far more obvious to the workers than to the intellectuals. In the workers' mentalities there is nothing in common; the two classes do not speak the same language. The labor unions emphatically assert today that no alliance could possibly exist between them and the politicians of the middle classes. This assertion is strictly true.

It was always so, and, no doubt, this is why popular democracy never has been defended by great thinkers, from Plato's times to our own.

Natural Inequalities and Democratic Equalization

The difficulty of reconciling democratic equalization with natural inequalities constitutes one of the most difficult problems of the present hour. We know what are the desires of democracy. Let us see what nature replies to these demands.

The democratic ideas which have so often shaken the world from the heroic ages of Greece to modern times are always clashing with natural inequalities. Some observers held, with Helvetius, that the inequality among men is created by education.

As a matter of fact, nature does not know such a thing as equality. She distributes unevenly genius, beauty, health, vigor, intelligence and all the qualities conferring on their possessors a superiority over their fellows. No theory can alter these discrepancies, so that democratic doctrines will remain confined to words until the laws of heredity consent to level the capacities of men.

Can we suppose that societies ever will succeed in establishing artificially the equality refused by nature? A few theorists have believed for a long time that education might effect a general leveling. Many years of experience have shown the depth of this illusion.

It would not, however, be impossible for a triumphant socialism to establish equality for a time by rigorously eliminating all superior individuals. One can easily foresee what would become of a people that had suppressed its best individuals while surrounded by other nations progressing by means of their best individuals.

Not only does nature not know equality, but since the beginning of the ages she always has realized progress by means of successive differentiations—that is to say, increasing inequalities. These alone could raise the obscure cell of the early geological periods to the superior being whose inventions were to change the face of the earth.

The same phenomenon is to be observed in societies. The forms of democracy which select the better elements of the popular classes finally result in the creation of an intellectual aristocracy, a result contrary to the dream of the pure theorists wanting to reduce the superior elements of society to the level of the inferior elements.

On the side of natural laws, which is hostile to theories of equality, are the conditions of modern progress. Science and industry demand more and more considerable intellectual efforts, so that mental inequalities and the differences of social condition which spring from them cannot but become accentuated. We therefore observe this striking phenomenon: as laws and institutions seek to level individuals, the progress of civilization tends still further to differentiate them. From the peasant to the feudal baron the intellectual difference was not so great; but from the workingman to the engineer it is immense and is increasing daily.

Ability being the principal factor of progress, the capable of each class rise while the mediocre remain stationary or sink. What could laws do in the face of such inevitable necessities?

In vain do the incapable pretend that, representing number, they also represent force. Deprived of the superior brains by whose researches all workers profit, they would speedily sink into poverty and anarchy.

The Results of Democratic Revolution

The Jacobin spirit . . . always endeavors to impose by force illusions which it regards as the truth. . . .

The Jacobin religion—above all in its socialist form —has all the power of the ancient faiths over feeble minds. Blinded by their faith, they believe that reason is their guide, but are really actuated solely by their passions and their dreams.

The evolution of democratic ideas has thus produced not only the political results already mentioned but also a considerable effect upon the mentality of modern man.

If the ancient dogmas have long been exhausted of their power, the theories of democracy are far from having lost theirs and we see the consequences increasing daily. One of the chief results has been a general hatred of superiority. This hatred of whatever surpasses the average in social fortune or intelligence is today general in all classes, from the working class to the upper strata of the bourgeoisie. The results are envy, detraction, a love of attack, of scornful wit, of persecution, and a habit of attributing all actions to low motives, of refusing to believe in probity, disinterestedness and intelligence. . . .

"There is a low demagogic instinct," writes M. Bourdeau, "without any moral inspiration, which dreams of pulling humanity down to the lowest level, and for which any superiority, even of culture, is an offense against society. . . . it is the sentiment of ignoble equality which animated the Jacobin butchers when they cut off the head of a Lavoisier or a Chénier."

This hatred of superiority, the most prominent element in the modern progress of socialism, is not the only characteristic of the new spirit created by democratic ideas. Other consequences, although indirect, are not less profound. Such, for example, are the progress of *statism,* the diminution of the power of the middle classes, the increasing activity of financiers, the conflict of the classes, the vanishing of the old social constraints, and the degradation of morality.

The Craving for Reforms

The craze for reforms imposed suddenly by means of decrees is one of the most disastrous concepts of the Jacobin spirit, one of the formidable legacies left by the Revolution. . . .

One of the psychological causes of this intense thirst for reforms arises from the difficulty of determining the real causes of the evils complained of. The need of explanation creates fictitious causes of the simplest nature. Therefore the remedies also appear simple.

For forty years we have incessantly been enacting reforms, each of which is a little revolution in itself. . . .

No one yet seems to understand that individuals and their methods, not regulations, make the value of a people. The efficacious reforms are not the revolutionary ones but the trifling ameliorations of every day accumulated in the course of time. The great social changes, like the great geological changes, are effected by the daily addition of minute causes. . . .

Unhappily, the progress in little things which by their total make up the greatness of a nation is rarely apparent, produces no impression on the public, and cannot serve the interests of politicians at elections. These latter care nothing for such matters and permit the accumulation, in countries subject to their influence, of the little successive disorganizations which finally result in great downfalls. . . .

Monarchies and democracies differ far more in form than in substance. It is only the variable mentality of men that varies their effects. All the discussions about various systems of government are really of no interest, for these have no special virtue in themselves. Their value always will depend on that of the people governed. A people achieves great and rapid progress when it discovers that it is the sum of the personal efforts of each individual and not the system of government that determines the rank of a nation in the world.

New Forms of Democratic Belief
The Conflict Between Capital and Labor

On all sides we see the birth of formidable problems which the harangues of politicians will never resolve. Among these new problems one of the most complicated will be that of the conflict between labor and capital. It is becoming acute in even such a country of tradition as England. Working men are ceasing to respect the collective contracts which formerly constituted their charter, strikes are declared for insignificant motives, and unemployment and pauperism are attaining disquieting proportions.

In America these strikes would finally have affected all industries had not the very excess of the evil created a remedy. During the last ten years, the industrial leaders organized great employers' federations which have become powerful enough to force the workers to submit to arbitration. . . .

These conflicts between workers and employers of the same nation will be rendered still more acute by the increasing economic struggle between the Asians, whose needs are small and who can therefore produce manufactured articles at very low prices, and the Europeans, whose needs are many. For twenty-five years I have laid stress on this point.

The Evolution of the Working Classes and the Syndicalist Movement

The most important democratic problem of the day will perhaps result from the recent development of the working class engendered by the syndicalist or trades-union movement.

The aggregation of similar interests known as syndicalism has rapidly assumed such enormous development in all countries that it may be called worldwide. Certain corporations have budgets comparable to those of small states. . . .

This extension of the labor movement in all countries shows that it is not, like socialism, a dream of utopian theorists, but the result of economic necessities. In its aim, its means of action and its tendencies, syndicalism presents no basic kinship with socialism. . . .

Socialism would obtain possession of all industries and have them managed by the state, which would distribute its products equally among citizens. Syndicalism, on the other hand, would entirely eliminate the action of the state and divide society into small professional groups which would be self-governing.

Although despised by the syndicalists and violently attacked by them, the socialists are trying to ignore the conflict, but it is rapidly becoming too obvious to be concealed. The political influence which the socialists still possess among the syndicalists will soon escape their grasp.

If syndicalism is everywhere increasing at the expense of socialism, it is because . . . it synthesizes certain needs born of the specialization of modern industry. . . .

In France its success has not yet been as great as elsewhere. Having taken the revolutionary form . . . it has already fallen, at least for the time being, into the hands of the anarchists, who care as little for syndicalism as for any sort of organization, and are simply using the new doctrine in an attempt to destroy modern society. Socialists, syndicalists, and anarchists, although directed by entirely different conceptions, are thus collaborating in the same eventual aim—the violent suppression of the ruling classes and the pillage of their wealth.

The syndicalist [or trade-union] movement does not in any way derive from the principles of the [French] Revolution. On many points it is entirely in contradiction with it. Syndicalism represents rather a return to certain forms of collective organization similar to the guilds or corporations proscribed by the Revolution. It thus constitutes one of those federations which the Revolution condemned. It entirely rejects the state centralization which the Revolution established.

Syndicalism cares nothing for the democratic principles of liberty, equality and fraternity. The syndicalists [trade unions] demand an absolute discipline of their members which eliminates all liberty.

Not being strong enough yet to exercise mutual tyranny, the unions so far profess sentiments of respect for one another which might by a stretch be called fraternal. But as soon as they are sufficiently powerful, when their contrary interests will necessarily come into conflict, as during the syndicalist period of the old Italian republics—Florence and Siena, for example—the present fraternity will speedily be forgotten and equality will be replaced by the despotism of the most powerful.

The new power is increasing very rapidly and finds

governments powerless before it, able to defend themselves only by yielding to every demand—an odious policy which may serve for the moment but which heavily compromises the future. . . .

Anarchy and the social conflicts resulting from democratic ideas are today impelling some governments toward an unforeseen course of evolution which will end by leaving them only a nominal power. . . .

The governments of democratic countries today consist of the representatives elected by universal suffrage. They vote laws and appoint and dismiss ministers chosen by themselves who are temporarily entrusted with executive power. These ministers are naturally often replaced, since a vote will do it. Those who follow them, belonging to a different party, will govern according to different principles.

It might at first seem that a country thus pulled to and fro by various influences could have no continuity or stability. But in spite of all these conditions of instability, a democratic government like that of France works with fair regularity. How can one explain such a phenomenon? Its interpretation, which is very simple, results from the fact that the ministers who have the appearance of governing really govern the country only to a very limited extent. Their power, strictly limited and circumscribed, is exercised principally in speeches which are hardly noticed and in a few inorganic measures.

But behind the ministers' superficial power, which

is without force or authority and is the plaything of every demand made on it, there is an anonymous power secretly at work whose might is continually increasing —that of the administrations [bureaucracies]. Possessing traditions, a hierarchy and continuity, they are a power against which the ministers, as they quickly learn, are incapable of struggling. Responsibility is so divided within the administrative machine that a minister may never find himself opposed by any person of importance. His momentary impulses are checked by a network of regulations, customs and decrees which are continually quoted to him and about which he knows so little that he dare not infringe them.

This diminution of power in democratic governments can only become aggravated. One of the most constant laws of history is that . . . immediately after any one class has become preponderant—the nobles, army, clergy or the people—it speedily tends to enslave others. Such were the Roman armies which finally appointed and overthrew the emperors; such were the clergy, against whom the kings of old could hardly struggle; such were the states-general which, at the moment of the Revolution, speedily absorbed all the powers of government and supplanted the monarchy.

The caste of functionaries is destined to furnish fresh proof of the truth of this law. Preponderant already, they are beginning to speak loudly, to make threats, and even to indulge in strikes, such as that of the postmen, which was quickly followed by that of the government railway employees. The administrative power forms a little state within a state, and if its present rate of revolution continues, it will soon constitute the only power in the state. Under a socialist government there would be no other power. All our revolutions would then have resulted in stripping the king of his powers and throne in order to bestow them upon the irresponsible, anonymous, and despotic class of government clerks.

To foresee the issue of all the conflicts which threaten to cloud the future is impossible. We must steer clear of pessimism and optimism; all we can say is that necessity will always finally bring things to an equilibrium. The world pursues its way without bothering itself with our speeches, and sooner or later we manage to adapt ourselves to the variations of our environment. The problem is to do so without too much friction, and above all to resist the chimerical concepts of dreamers. Always powerless to reorganize the world, they have often contrived to upset it.

Athens, Rome, Florence, and many other cities which formerly shone in history were victims of these terrible theorists. The results of their influence have always been the same—anarchy, dictatorship and decadence.

But such lessons will not affect the numerous Catilines of the present day. They do not yet see that the movements unchained by their ambitions threaten to submerge them. All these utopians have awakened impossible hopes in the mind of the crowd, excited their appetites, and weakened the dikes that were erected slowly during the centuries to restrain them.

The struggle of blind multitudes against the elect is one of the continuous facts of history, and the triumph of popular sovereignties without counterpoise has already marked the end of more than one civilization. The elect create; the plebeians destroy. As soon as the former lose their hold, the latter begin their destructive work.

The great civilizations have prospered only by dominating their lower elements. It is not only in Greece that anarchy, dictatorship, invasion and finally loss of independence resulted from the despotism of a democracy. Individual tyranny is always born of collective tyranny. It ended the first cycle of the greatness of Rome; the barbarians finished off the second.

Conclusions

The French Revolution is an inexhaustible mine of psychological documents. No period in the life of humanity has presented such a mass of experience accumulated in so short a time.

On each page of this great drama we have found numerous applications of the principles expounded in my various works concerning the transitory mentality of crowds, the permanent soul of the peoples, the actions of beliefs, the influence of mystic, affective and collective elements, and the conflict between the various forms of logic.

The [French] Revolutionary Assemblies illustrate all the known laws of the psychology of crowds. Impulsive and timid, they are dominated by a small number of leaders, and usually act in a sense contrary to the wishes of their individual members.

The Royalist Constituent Assembly destroyed an ancient monarchy; the humanitarian Legislative Assembly allowed the massacres of September. The same pacific body led France into the most formidable military campaigns.

There were similar contradictions during the Convention. The immense majority of its members abhorred violence. Sentimental philosophers, they exalted equality, fraternity and liberty, yet ended by exerting the most terrible despotism.

The same contradictions appeared during the Directorate. Extremely moderate in their intentions at the outset, the Assemblies were continually carrying out bloodthirsty *coups d'état*. They wished to reestablish religious peace, and finally sent thousands of priests to prison. They wished to repair the ruins covering France but succeeded only in adding to them.

Thus there always was a complete contradiction between the individual wills of men of the revolutionary period and the deeds of the Assemblies of which they were units. The truth is that they obeyed invisible forces of which they were not the masters. Believing that they

acted in the name of pure reason, they were really subject to mystic, affective and collective influences incomprehensible to them and which we are only today
beginning to understand.

Intelligence has progressed in the course of the ages
and has opened a marvelous outlook to man, although
his character, the real foundation of his mind and the
sure motive of his actions, has scarcely changed. Overthrown one moment, it reappears the next. Human nature must be accepted as it is.

The founders of the Revolution did not resign themselves to the facts of human nature. For the first time in
the history of humanity, they tried to transform men
and society in the name of reason.

Never was any undertaking begun with such oppor-
tunities for success. The theorists, who claimed to be
carrying it out, had a power in their hands greater
than that of any despot. Yet despite this power, despite
the success of the armies, despite Draconian laws and
repeated *coups d'état,* the Revolution merely heaped
ruin upon ruin and ended in dictatorship.

Such an attempt was not useless, since experience
is necessary to the education of the people. Without
the Revolution, it would have been difficult to prove
that pure reason does not enable us to change human
nature, and, consequently, that no society can be rebuilt by the will of legislators.

Although the lesson of the Revolution was extremely
categorical, many impractical spirits, hallucinated by

their dreams, are hoping to recommence it. Socialism, the modern synthesis of this hope, would be a regression to lower forms of evolution, for it would paralyze the greatest sources of our activity. By replacing individual initiative and responsibility with collective initiative and responsibility, mankind would descend several rungs on the ladder of human values.

Part VII

Aphorisms of
Present Times

(Aphorismes du Temps Présent)

First edition published in Paris by E. Flammarion, 1913.

Part One

Affective Life

I
Character and Personality

One does not behave according to one's intelligence but according to one's character.

The self is composed of an aggregate of heterogeneous ancestral elements. Unity of self is as fictitious as unity of an army.

To attribute to others the identical sentiments that guide oneself is never to understand others.

Thanks to the suggestion of habit, men know what to say, do and think every day.

Important works rarely are the result of one great effort but of an accumulation of little efforts.

Vanity is a powerful source of satisfaction for fools. It permits them to substitute for qualities they never will have, the conviction of always having had them.

To belong to a school of thought is to lose one's personality; not to belong to one is to abdicate all possibility of prestige.

Sentiments are the basis of existence. The day when cold reason would replace the devotion, pity, love and illusions that guide us, all the mainsprings of activity would be broken.

II
The Affective and the Rational

The evolution of sentiments is independent of will. No one can love or hate at will.

In matters of sentiment, illusion quickly creates certitude.

The strength of sentimental evidence is that it doesn't take rational evidence into account.

What is done through pride is superior to what is accomplished from duty.

Affective, mystical and collective influences are the great commanders of history.

To demonstrate that a thing is rational doesn't always prove that it is reasonable.

III
Pleasure and Pain

Man knows only two absolute certainties: pleasure and pain. They orient all his individual and social life.

Above all, happiness is hope of realization not yet attained.

The real length of life doesn't depend on the number of one's days but on the diversity of sensations accumulated during those days.

IV
Feminine Psychology

Intuition often is superior to reason. It permits poorly reasoned women to predict things incomprehensible to well-reasoned men.

According to various fields of activity, woman is inferior or superior to man. She rarely is his equal.

A woman never forgives a man for guessing what she thinks behind what she says.

To dominate or be dominated is the only alternative for the feminine soul.

Women reproach men for not understanding them, but where are those of different mentality who ever understood one another?

In love, one demands words for fear of hearing thoughts.

Love elevates or degrades; it never permits us to remain ourselves.

To try to hold on to a dying love is like trying to slow down the passage of time.

V
Opinions

Our opinions often represent little beliefs in process of formation and, as a result, not yet stabilized.

The majority of men's opinions are founded not on deduction but on hate, sympathy and hope.

Environment creates our opinions. Only passion and self-interest change them.

It requires a very independent mind to arrive at five or six personal opinions in the course of a lifetime.

To dispute the worth of an affective or mystical opinion is to strengthen it.

Crowds don't create opinion but give it its strength. A popular opinion quickly becomes contagious.

The power of public opinion is irresistible. One can only dominate it by creating it; if one doesn't know how to create it, one must submit to it.

VI
Words and Slogans

The more a word goes into general usage, the more it takes on different meanings according to the mentality of those who use it.

The incomprehension ruling relations among beings

of different race, social situation and sex is irreducible because the same words evoke different ideas to them. One can therefore say that in reality they do not speak the same language.

In politics, things are less important than their names. To disguise even the most absurd ideas with well-chosen words often is enough to gain their acceptance.

With many men, words take precedence over thought. They only know what they think after having heard what they said.

VII
Persuasion

The art of persuasion has five chapters: affirmation; repetition; prestige; suggestion; contagion.

Mental contagion is the surest agent of the propagation of opinions and beliefs. Political convictions are not founded by other means and are afterward given a rational aspect in order to justify them.

If general beliefs are almost always wrong, it is because they represent a single individual's illusion spread by contagion.

Repeated often enough, the most disastrous theories end by being incorporated into our subconscious and become a driving power for action.

It always is better to obtain something by suggestion than by constraint.

It is easier to rule people by exciting their emotions than by protecting their interests.

VIII
Prestige

He who possesses prestige has no need of force.

Prestige can replace force, but force cannot replace prestige.

Force can command obedience, but prestige removes even the idea of disobedience.

No voluntary obedience without respect; no respect without prestige.

An error crowned with prestige always will be more powerful than a truth without prestige.

Governments and people who lose their prestige soon lose all else.

Part Two

I
The Soul of Races

There are no pure races except among primitives. Among civilized peoples, the repetition of crossings and similarity of environment has created new historic races analogous to pure races.

The psychological characteristics of an historic race are as stable as its anatomical characteristics. They are transmitted by heredity with regularity and persistence.

The history of a people is the recital of its efforts to stabilize its soul and thus emerge from barbarism.

The strength of a people resides less in the power of its armed forces than in its community of sentiments engendered by the solidity of its national soul. The national soul of the Romans enabled them to rule the world. When they lost their soul, their power vanished.

Regressive evolution being much faster than ascendant evolution, people take centuries to acquire a certain mental structure and sometimes lose it very fast.

A civilized people is a crowd whose soul was stabilized during the very slow ancestral accumulations.

Crowds make revolutions; the soul of a race shortens the duration.

Every historic race and every phase of its life imply certain institutions, certain morals, certain arts, certain philosophies and no others. No people has adopted a foreign civilization without entirely transforming it.

To try to impose our institutions, our customs and

our laws on the natives of a colony is to try to substitute the past of one race for that of another.

Only heredity can struggle against heredity. The crossing of unequal individuals disaggregates the ancestral soul of the race. Many nations have perished for not having understood this.

Patriotism represents the synthesis of the aspirations of the national soul.

The half-breed is a man who floats among contrary ancestral impulses of intelligence, morality and character.

A population of half-breeds is ungovernable.

The past never dies. It lives in us and constitutes the surest guide of the conduct of individuals and of people. The soul of the living is above all composed of the thoughts of the dead.

The dead are terribly tyrannical.

To create ideas which influence men is to put a little of oneself into the life of one's descendants.

II
The Soul of Crowds

A man who is part of a crowd ceases to be himself. His conscious personality vanishes into the unconscious soul of the crowd. He loses all critical spirit, all ability to reason and returns to primitiveness.

A crowd is an amorphous being incapable of will or action without a leader. Since the crowd's sentiments are exaggerated, it demands that the leader's be too.

It is much easier to influence a crowd than an individual.

It is its sense of power and irresponsibility that gives the crowd its intolerance and excessive arrogance.

The crowd must have a fetish—a personage, doctrine or formula.

The mysticism that saturates a crowd is what makes it attribute mystical power to a political formula or to a hero seducing it.

Crowds always are impressed by power, only rarely by goodness.

Crowds respect only the strong. Disdain for the weak is their law.

III
The Soul of Assemblies

Great assemblies possess the same characteristics as crowds: mediocre intellectual level, excessive excitability, sudden furors, complete intolerance and servile obedience to leaders.

The mediocre man augments his worth by belonging to a group; the superior man diminishes it.

The only way to influence the individuals in a group is first to influence its leaders.

A brutal daring minority will always lead a fearful, irresolute majority.

The fate of a people depends much more on their character than on their intelligence.

For a people not to have had a past, as in the United States, is at one and the same time a strength and a weakness.

Crowds generally prefer equality in servitude to liberty.

When the social brakes restraining the multitude's instincts are removed, they return very quickly to their ancestral barbarism.

To give in once to the crowd is to make it conscious of its strength and to condemn oneself to give in to it always.

IV
The Life of Peoples

A people's ancestral soul dominates all its evolution. Political upheavals modify only the manifestation of this soul.

No people can try to break abruptly with its fore-bears without profoundly affecting the course of its history.

Latin nations quickly grow more tired of liberty than of servitude.

People who have not acquired an internal discipline are condemned to submit to an external discipline.

The elite of people create its progress; the middle classes furnish its strength.

No people with a fast growing population can remain pacifist. It ends by invading neighbors whose population is stationary.

An advanced civilization retains all the residue of the successive steps through which it has passed. The cave man and Attila's barbarians still have their representatives among us.

The civilization of a people is the outward clothing of its soul, the visible expression of the invisible forces that control it.

A strong faith renders a people unconquerable only for so long as they do not face a stronger faith.

A people's progress is determined neither by its governments nor its revolutions but by the sum of efforts of the individuals who compose it.

Peoples, like all living beings, disappear when they have become so stabilized by a long past that they are incapable of adapting themselves to new conditions of existence.

V
Institutions and Laws

Since man is incapable of living in society without tyranny, the most acceptable is that of laws.

Political institutions do not create the sentiments of a people; institutions are created by their sentiments.

Individual tyranny is near when groups are able to avoid the law.

It is easy to remake the laws of a nation on paper, but this does not remake its soul.

VI
Justice

Nature ignores justice. Equity is a creation of man.

Justice begins only at the moment when one has the power to impose it.

Law and justice play no role in the relations of peoples of unequal strength.

One cannot contrast law and power, because power and law are only labels. Law is power that endures.

VII
Morals

Moral laws are not fictitious entities but imperious necessities.

Morals represent the synthesis of the social needs of an epoch. Owing to the sole fact that a society wants to exist, it is obliged to have an irreducible criterion of good and evil.

No civilization can endure without morals.

To try to base morals on reason, as so many philosophers do, is a dangerous illusion. Morals deprived of affective or mystical support are without duration and strength.

Environment and example are the two great generators of morals.

It sometimes takes generations for a people to acquire morals and only a few years for it to lose them.

The morals of a people represent their scale of values.

The minimum possible morals are those codified by law and imposed by the police. The moment that the minimum is no longer respected, anarchy begins.

One can consider it to be a grave symptom of decadence when the morality of the ruling classes falls below that of those who are ruled.

Whenever humanitarianism flourishes, morals decline.

Crime in any nation grows with the development of humanitarianism. Ceaselessly limiting repression, humanitarianism reduces inhibiting action and punishment.

To excuse evil is to multiply it.

The more a people possesses internal discipline, and therefore a stable morality, the higher it rises in civilization.

Peoples disappear quickly from history when their morality begins to come apart.

VIII
The Ideal

Revolutions and anarchy represent the ransom a people must pay for a change of ideal.

One can do nothing for a man whose ideal, like that of the Russian revolutionaries, is to sacrifice his life for a belief.

People whose ideals are strong and needs meager always will triumph over those whose needs are great and ideals mediocre.

To destroy the ideal of an individual, a class, or a people is to take away all that made for cohesion, greatness and motivation for action.

To devote longtime effort toward setting up an ideal

and just as much effort in destroying it is the life cycle of a people.

IX
Gods

It is not necessary to multiply gods. Under various names, man has adored during all the ages only one divinity—hope.

Man sometimes changes the names of his gods but never can do without them. Mysticism seems to be an indestructible need of the spirit.

Mystical logic can dominate affective logic to the point of nullifying the instinct for self-preservation.

Gods and heroes condense people's obscure aspirations into luminous synthesis.

The religious spirit is independent of the dogmas feeding it. The Jacobins of the [Reign of] Terror and the priests of the [Spanish] Inquisition had exactly the same mentality.

Incapable of living without certitude, man always will prefer the most untenable beliefs to the most justified negations.

If atheism were to triumph, it would become a religion as intolerant as the old faiths.

Free thinking is often nothing but a belief that avoids the effort of thinking.

It always is imprudent to try to rationalize one's faith.

Religions constitute a force to use, never to combat.

People rarely survive the death of their gods.

X
The Arts

The birth of the arts always has preceded that of philosophy and the sciences. The offspring of affective and mystical needs prior to the age of reason, the arts can flourish in the times of barbarians.

Like politics, art is guided by a few leaders followed by a crowd of followers.

Mental contagion is so powerful in art that one can ascertain in an epoch a familiar air enabling recognition of the time of its creation.

Art is so subject to the influence of environment and race that there is not in all history, despite certain contrary appearances, a people able to adopt the arts of another people without transforming them.

Man, confined by nature to the ephemeral, dreams of the eternal. In raising temples and statues, he indulges in the illusion of having created things that never will perish.

The true artist creates even when he copies.

XI
Rites and Symbols

Rites and symbols—ceremonies, flags, holidays, wordly customs—dominate the individual will. They constitute the surest supports of religious and social life.

There is no place in society for someone who pretends to be emancipated from rites and disdains symbols.

It is only under the influence of rites and symbols that individual beliefs can take on a collective character.

Justice deprived of rites and symbols would no longer be justice.

A religious or political belief can be founded on faith but cannot endure without rites and symbols.

The power of rites is so great that they often survive long after the disappearance of the faith that gave birth to them.

The most independent, free thinking and skeptical of men voluntarily submit their existence to political, worldly and social rites depriving them of all real liberty.

Rites avoid man's uncertainties. Thanks to rites, he

knows without thinking what he should say and do in all circumstances.

The fundamental rites and symbols of a people are the creation of its dead.

Part Three

I
Rational Life
Belief and Knowledge

Knowledge establishes truths; belief incorporates our desires; that is why man always will prefer belief to knowledge.

Religions give our illusions, born of our desires, an appearance of reality. Science alone creates realities independent of our desires.

Reason is crushed against the wall of belief.

To create a belief is to create a new conscience generating new conduct.

The slightest change in people's beliefs modifies their destiny.

Whenever a question raises violently contradictory opinions, one can be sure that it belongs to the cycle of belief and not to that of knowledge.

Divergencies of rational origin are easily tolerated;

the antagonisms of belief are intolerant. Religious and political struggles always will be violent.

An hypothesis often is a belief mistaken for knowledge.

Rationally contradictory things are easily reconciled in a mind hypnotized by belief.

Not to believe things to be possible is to render them impossible. One of the strengths of faith is to ignore the impossible.

Man always has needed beliefs to orient his thoughts and guide his conduct. Neither philosophy nor science has been able so far to replace beliefs.

II
Instruction and Education

Education is the art of making the conscious flow into the unconscious.

Well educated, our unconscious is our slave and works for us. Badly educated, it becomes our master and acts against us.

It is strength of character and not instruction that gives man a strong internal defense. Deprived of that defense, he becomes the plaything of all circumstances.

To instruct is not to educate. Instruction enriches memory. Education creates useful reflexive impulses in man and teaches him to control his harmful ones.

It requires only a few years to instruct a barbarian but sometimes centuries to educate him.

To confine the mind to the artificial and render it incapable of observation is the sure result of teaching about the world only through books.

Science elevates or debases according to the mental terrain that receives it. Superior culture can be useful only to superior minds.

Too much instruction imposed on inferior mentalities confuses all their judgments. Half-rational, they lose their intuitive primitive qualities and become half-caste intellectuals.

Channeled by good methods, even the weakest intelligence can attain progress.

The educator should determine the aptitudes of each pupil which can be usefully developed. To leave to chance the choice of studies or careers is to make most men into mediocrities.

III
The Elites

The strength of a nation isn't measured by the number of the population but by the worth of its elites.

Created by the elite, civilization can progress only by it. Deprived of elites, a nation would soon fall into misery and anarchy.

The people are the great reservoir of energy in a country, but this energy cannot be used unless it is channeled by an elite.

One of the greatest illusions of democracy is to imagine that instruction equalizes men. It often serves only to emphasize their differentiation.

Our system of classical education creates an aristocracy of memory not having any relationship with judgment and intelligence.

Choice of a system of education is more important for a people than choice of government.

The inventions of genius always are personal. They spread by becoming collective.

Aristocracy has always taken on different forms: birth, talent or fortune. The world never has been able to do without an aristocracy.

Intellectual aristocracy must seem as unfair to the egalitarian crowd as the ancient nobility. Birth alone confers intellectual qualities in the same manner as it used to confer privileges.

The struggle of the blind multitude against the elites is an historical continuity. The triumph of the more numerous has marked the end of several civilizations.

Great civilizations prospered only by knowing how to dominate their inferior elements.

The elite create; the plebeians destroy.

IV
Philosophic Concepts

The logic of the universe is too different from our logic for us to hope to penetrate its secrets.

If we were to describe as a miracle all that is incomprehensible, the life of any being must be considered as a perpetual miracle.

The smallest living cell carries within itself an immense past and mysterious future.

Is the world created or uncreated, real or unreal, humanity durable or ephemeral? Philosophy, which used to try to answer such questions, nowadays renounces their solution.

Certain dangerous questions—where do we come from? where are we going?—ought not to be too much discussed in order to leave a cloud of doubt which doesn't blot out all hope.

Of the three possible concepts of life—optimistic, pessimistic and resigned—the last is perhaps the wisest but also the least motivating of action.

To revolt or to adapt oneself; there is no other choice in life.

Every phenomenon has its mystery. A mystery is the unknown soul of things.

V
Scientific Principles

Science is in reality man's revolt against nature, his effort to escape the blind forces that oppress him.

The supposed pre-established harmony of the universe probably is owing to the inevitable balance of the forces that compose it.

The most precise scientific laws are valid only for a limited portion of time and space.

The two great constants of the universe are resistance and movement. The first is composed of inertia, and the second of energy.

The terrain of science is known but represents only a little island in a boundless sea of things unknown.

Scientific achievements merely displace within the infinite the barriers separating us from the inaccessible.

Materialism is a pretended substitute for religions, but today matter has become as mysterious as the gods it replaces.

One of the superiorities of the savant over the ignoramus is that the savant senses where mystery begins.

Science creates more mysteries than it elucidates.

VI
Matter

Matter, which used to be regarded as inert and able only to store energy previously furnished to it, is on the contrary a colossal reservoir of energy—intra-atomic energy—capable of being spent spontaneously.

It is intra-atomic energy, freed during the disassociation of matter, from which there result most of the forces of the universe, notably electricity and solar heat.

Energy and matter are two aspects of the same thing. Matter represents a relatively stable form of intra-atomic energy. Heat, light, electricity, etc., represent unstable forms of the same energy.

Matter is transformed into diverse forms of energy, but doubtless it is unique to the origin of things that energy can transform itself into matter.

VII
Truth and Error

The need for certainty always has been greater than the need for truth.

The practical value of a truth is measured by the degree of belief it inspires.

Clothed seductively, error often wins acceptance as truth.

Truth is not an entity or commodity or utility but a necessity.

Before science, man knew only subjective truths; the role of savants was to create impersonal truths.

A truth is merely a tentative step along an endless road.

There are absolute truths in time but not in eternity.

The centuries transform most of our truths into errors.

Many men easily do without truth but none is strong enough to do without illusions.

It is in pursuing an illusion that man often has achieved progress he did not seek.

Error probably has rendered more services to man than truth.

VIII
Legend and History

History unfurls itself outside of reason and often against reason.

The mental life of each generation is derived from preceding generations.

Legend generally is truer than history. The former translates people's real feelings; the latter tells about happenings deformed by the narrator's mentality.

Psychological conflicts rule history. The great upheavals occur more because of conflicts of belief than opposition of interests.

The unreal still is the driving force of the world.

Part Four

I

Thought and Action

Action

Intelligence makes one think. Belief makes one act.

Had man begun to think before he acted, the cycle of history would have been ended long ago.

Only action reveals the nature of our intelligence and worth of our character.

To think is useful, but to act without too much thinking often is necessary. The great acts of heroism generally were due to men who didn't think first.

Thoughts, like all phenomena in life, are the result of unstable balances being ceaselessly transformed.

To know what one ought to do is not always to know what one is going to do.

II

Democratic Illusions

The word *democracy* signifies entirely different ideas to the crowd and to scholars.

Dominated by a need for equality, popular democracy repulses fraternity among the classes and doesn't give a fig for liberty. On the contrary, democracy among the intellectuals is avid for liberty and cares little for equality.

The true democrat is a member of a group who has no individuality outside his group.

Contrary to democratic ideas, the psychology of the collective entity called The People is much inferior to that of an isolated man.

Hatred of despotism and love of liberty always have been proclaimed by peoples well adjusted to despotism and very poorly to liberty.

Democratic ideas are among those ideas which are gladly imposed on others but rarely accepted for oneself.

The more the law proclaims equality, the more there develops the need for exterior signs of inequality.

The thirst for equality often is an expression of the desire to have inferiors and no superiors.

The artificial notion of equality has given rise to

hatred of all those superiorities that constitute the greatness of a nation.

The democracies will eventually succeed in replacing the intermittent wars between peoples with continual struggles between classes.

Nature does not recognize equality. The only progress has been through increasing inequalities.

Far from equalizing men, civilization accentuates their differentiation more and more each day.

By attributing imaginary powers to science, democracy makes a false god of it.

III
Socialist Illusions

Socialism, ultimate form of the principle of equality, is a mental state more than a doctrine.

Democracy and socialism, despite appearances, are separated by a profound abyss.

Socialism, which preaches the equalization of conditions, is in obvious opposition to the democracy of the intellectuals who pretend to be able to achieve the triumph of the more capable.

The hard-heartedness of certain capitalists and the weakness of their morality create many followers of socialism.

When the state tries to protect its citizens too much, they lose their habit of protecting themselves and as a result lose all initiative.

Most beliefs do not bring on disillusion because their paradise is in inaccessible regions. The weakness of socialism is that its paradise is located down here on earth.

The stingy happiness and equality in servitude promised by socialism do not form a strong enough ideal to impassion peoples for a very long time.

Because of its progress, modern civilization creates an ever-increasing mass of unadapted people always ready to struggle against it. They form the majority of socialists.

Wealth, which used to be the immobilization of capital, today depends on the rapidity of its circulation, and therefore on the intelligence that manipulates it.

IV
Pacifism and War

To live is to struggle. Struggle is universal. Non-combative beings would have made no progress.

If nature had not been pitiless toward the weak, the world would be peopled by monsters and no civilization would have taken place.

Only people with lots of cannons have the right to be pacifists.

To withdraw in the face of effort one believes to be useless is to renounce all success in advance.

Fear of being defeated increases the chances of defeat. An army persuaded of its superiority doubles its courage and chances of victory.

Individual courage is rarer than collective courage.

Economic interests lead people to long for peace, but their differences of feelings and beliefs always push them into war.

A truly pacifist people would quickly disappear from history.

V
Revolutions

The only lasting revolutions are those of thought.

Scientific revolutions are uniquely derived from reason; political and religious revolutions derive from affective, mystical and collective elements.

Scientific revolutions transform people's lives much more than political revolutions.

Revolutions, like wars, represent the externalization of conflicts between psychological forces.

The really miserable man is one persuaded that his condition is miserable.

Mental contagion is the most powerful factor in a revolution.

The majority of men want to be led, not to revolt.

Among certain men, revolution is a mental state. No concession could appease it.

The beginning of revolution generally arises from the ending of beliefs.

VI
Popular Governments

That which is called popular government really is that of a few leaders.

To be guided by wrong but popular opinions is the imperative condition of all democratic governments.

Inflation, humanitarianism and fear always are the great factors in the conduct of democratic governments.

Popular government is dominated by too many passions to be equitable or tolerant. It can be maintained only by increasingly despotic methods.

Limited by fear of responsibility, individual despotism always is less oppressive than collective despotism, which always is irresponsible.

Individual tyranny is easily overthrown. Against collective tyranny, the oppressed have no force.

What one detests in a tyranny is not always tyranny itself but the individuals who exercise it.

The worst tyrants are easily accepted for so long as they remain anonymous.

No popular government is possible without a preponderance of the Jacobin mentality.

Narrowmindedness, strong passions, intense mysticism, incapacity to reason well, are the principal components of the Jacobin soul.

The Jacobin is not a rationalist but a believer. Far from edifying his belief with reason, he seeks to mold reason to his belief.

Group politics always are of inferior order. Popular governments can have no other.

The first task of a revolution is to destroy the old aristocracy; the second is to create a new one.

The crimes of kings are but little compared with those of the people.

In the eyes of the multitude, the modern state has inherited the mystical powers incarnated in Divine will.

The weaker a government, the stronger its bureaucracy.

Any people ceaselessly clamoring for equality ends by accepting servitude.

All politics is confined to two rules: to know and to foresee.

A government is not the creator of an epoch but is created by it.

Atomic physics, living cells, human entities remain a mere ineffectual dust for so long as directing forces do not channel their actions.

The real strength of a government resides less in its force than in the voluntary submission of those who obey it.

Individual and collective tyranny are the only forms of government discovered since the beginnings of history. The second always is the harsher.

The effects of political measures not being subject to prediction, the mania for great reforms is extremely dangerous for a people.

To deem a happening to be inevitable is to turn it into a fatality.

As soon as a class is no longer sure of its rights—the

nobles formerly, the middle class today—they soon lose them.

VII
Political Psychology

Without knowledge of the psychology of races, people, individuals and crowds, politics never will be understood.

A society is the aggregate of opposing forces which must be balanced. When balance is upset, anarchy begins.

In political life as in individual life, anxieties which can be expressed are far less important than those which cannot.

To overthrow a tyranny is not to create liberty.

The danger of autocracy doesn't reside in the autocrat but in the thousands of individuals sharing his power and individually becoming little despots.

Many political errors derive from ideas theoretically rational.

In politics it is less dangerous to lack controlling ideas than to have false ones.

More governments fall because of their own faults than from enemy attack.

The despotism of the living would perhaps be limitless were it not for that of the dead.

VIII
The Art of Governing

No society is possible without the principle of authority, in the same manner as there is no river without banks.

The surest way to destroy the principle of authority is for each one to talk of rights and not responsibilities. All men are ready to talk of the former and are little preoccupied with the latter.

One must govern people not only according to their material needs but also to their dreams.

Moral strength cannot be fought with laws or even armies.

To lead men one must not forget that their affective self and intellectual self do not come from the same evolution and scarcely influence each other.

To use people's affective and mystical impulses as a means of action while trying to give them a rational orientation is the secret of the art of governing.

One must never share the passions of men being led but one must know what they are.

A government should avoid persecutions. They always are more useful to the persecuted than to the persecutors.

The role of the scholar is to destroy chimeras, that of the statesman is to make use of them.

When a government follows instead of creates opinion, it ceases to be master.

One can easily disaggregate the soul of a crowd, but one is powerless against the permanent soul of a race.

To procrastinate in order to gain time for preparation, as Machiavelli advised, is very wise; to procrastinate in order to let chance shape the course of events is very dangerous.

Discontent always is the motivation of effort; a man too content makes no progress.

A government must erect moral boundaries before they become indispensable. When they become so, it is too late to raise them.

As soon as it becomes evident that necessity demands surrender, one must not wait for the moment when it becomes impossible not to surrender.

Always to give in to threats and acts of violence is to persuade the popular soul that it is enough to threaten or pillage in order to be obeyed.

No appeasement will avoid necessary battles. It only makes them more costly and lengthy.

A government that constantly instigates riots perishes by riots.

If people cannot be governed by true ideas, one must become resigned to governing them by ideas believed to be true.

In a statesman, common sense and good character often are more useful than genius.

A society cannot last without stable ideas; and an individual cannot progress without flexible ones.

The future is laden with the past; to foresee, that is to predict, one must always look back.

To foresee is useful; to take precautions more so. To foresee is to eliminate future surprises; to take precaution is to prevent their effects.

A statesman without foresight is the creator of disastrous fatalities.

Index

This book was linotype set in the Times Roman series of type. The face was designed to be used in the news columns of the *London Times*. The *Times* was seeking a type face that would be condensed enough to accommodate a substantial number of words per column without sacrificing readability and still have an attractive, contemporary appearance. This design was an immediate success. It is used in many periodicals throughout the world and is one of the most popular text faces presently in use for book work.

Book design by Design Center, Inc., Indianapolis, Indiana
Typography by Weimer Typesetting Co., Inc., Indianapolis, Indiana
Printed by LithoCrafters, Inc., Chelsea, Michigan